Collins

KS3 Revision History

History

KS3

Revision Guide

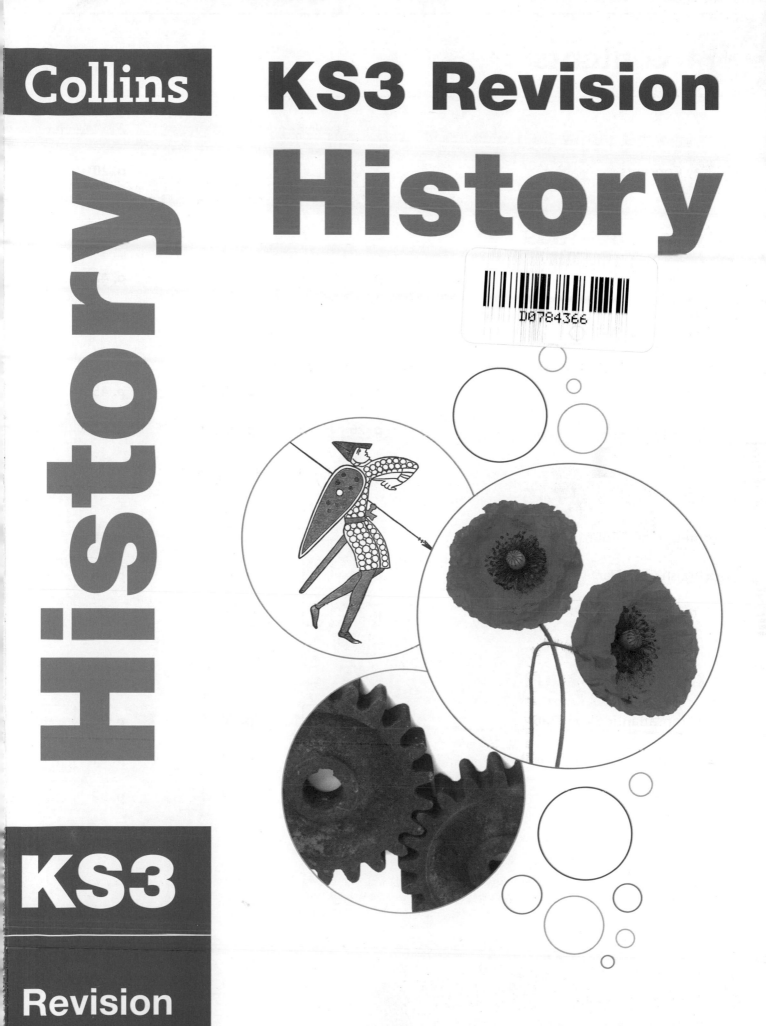

D0784366

**Philippa Birch, Steve McDonald
and Rachelle Pennock**

Contents

	Revise	Practise	Review

Contents

	Revise	Practise	Review

The Norman Conquest 1

You must be able to:

- Explain why the Norman Conquest was important in English history
- Describe how William the Conqueror won the Battle of Hastings
- Explain the changes made by the feudal system.

What was the Norman Conquest?

- In 1066, major change happened in England.
- The Saxons (originally from Germany) were defeated in battle by a ruler from Normandy in France, who became William I, known as the Conqueror.
- This was the last successful invasion of England.
- Under William the Conqueror, the Norman French became the new rulers of England.
- They took control of the land and the Church. They introduced a new way of organising the country called the feudal system.
- This change brought about the start of the Middle Ages in England, a period of history that would last for 500 years.

> **Key Point**
>
> Normandy was an area of northern France settled by people from Norway and Denmark, known as Normans from the word 'Norsemen'.

How did William Win the Battle of Hastings in 1066?

- The beginning of Norman rule in England began with their victory at the Battle of Hastings on 14 October 1066.
- When the English king, Edward the Confessor, died on 5 January 1066, Harold became the new Saxon English king.
- William of Normandy felt he had a claim to the English throne as his sister was married to Edward, and he said Edward had promised him the crown in 1051.
- William was supported by the Pope, who was head of the Christian Church in Europe.
- William invaded England by crossing the Channel from Normandy
- At the same time Harald Hardrada, King of Norway and Denmark, invaded northern England from Denmark.
- The Saxon English king, Harold, marched his army to the north of England to fight Harald Hardrada first.
- Harold defeated the Danes at Stamford Bridge in Yorkshire and then marched all the way south to fight William near Hastings.
- At the Battle of Hastings the Saxons fought well but their king, Harold, was killed.
- William of Normandy won the battle, marched on towards London and on 25 December 1066, he was crowned King William I.

William the Conqueror.

- A description of the battle was embroidered on cloth. It is called the Bayeux Tapestry, after the town in Normandy where it was made.
- The tapestry shows the main events of William's invasion of England and the Battle of Hastings. It was made over a decade after the battle.

Battle scene from the Bayeux Tapestry.

What was the Feudal System?

- The biggest change the Normans made in England was to introduce a new way of organising society, known as the feudal system.
- Under the feudal system King William I owned all the land in England.
- The King kept one-quarter of the land for his own use and gave the rest to his main supporters, barons and bishops.
- About 200 barons and bishops controlled three-quarters of England's land. They gave land to about 400 knights, who gave service to their barons in times of war.
- Most of the work in England was done by 1.5 million peasants. They were allowed small plots of land. In return they had to work for the baron when required.
- These peasants were called villeins. They employed poorer peasants called bordars and cottars.
- The feudal system meant that power in England was centred on the King and his barons and bishops. Most Saxons lost their land.

> **Key Point**
>
> Villeins were farm labourers or peasants who had to work several days each year for their baron in return for small plots of land.

> **Quick Test**
>
> 1. In what year was the Battle of Hastings?
> 2. Who was the King of the Saxons at this time?
> 3. Of which English king did William claim to be a distant relative?
> 4. What is the name of the famous tapestry that depicts the Battle of Hastings?
> 5. What is the name given to the system for organising society introduced by the Normans?

The Norman Conquest 2

You must be able to:

- Describe the rebellions against William the Conqueror
- Explain why castles helped the Normans to gain control
- Explain why the Domesday Book was important.

How did William Use Castles to Control England?

- When William I became king he established control of England.
- In England there were 1.5 million Saxon English and only 10 000 Normans.
- The Saxons did not want to be ruled by the French.
- There were rebellions by Saxons across England, including a rebellion in northern England in 1069.
- The most serious rebellion took place in eastern England, in an area known as the Fens. A Saxon lord, Hereward the Wake, fought the Normans for over a decade after 1066 before he was defeated.
- William kept control through building castles across England.
- Norman castles followed a standard pattern:
  - A small hill was created called a motte and this was surrounded by a wooden fence and a moat.
  - An outer area, called a bailey, was also surrounded by a wooden fence. This contained housing. Later the wooden fences were replaced by stone.
- Castles were the homes of lords and knights.
- The castles were easy to defend and showed the Saxon English that the Normans were in control.

> **Key Point**
>
> Motte and bailey is the type of castle built across England by the Normans as a way to keep control.

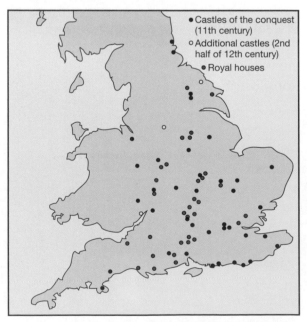

Locations of Norman castles by the end of the 12th century.

● Castles of the conquest (11th century)
○ Additional castles (2nd half of 12th century)
● Royal houses

Durham Castle is an example of a Norman castle.

The Domesday Book 1086

- In the winter of 1085–86 William I did something extraordinary that had never been done before. He made a survey of all the land in England and recorded it in a book, the Domesday Book.
- William sent officials around the country to ask questions about who owned land and what the land was worth.
- All answers were double checked on a second visit.
- Over 1300 places were visited.
- Normally six villagers and their leader, known as a reeve, were asked the questions.
- The Domesday Book mentions all of England's villages and records the value of their land.
- This gave William information about the wealth of his kingdom. It also showed the wealth of each of his lords and bishops.
- This was important because it showed William how much tax he could claim from each lord and bishop.

> **Revise**

> **Key Point**

The vast majority of English people lived in villages. That is why the Domesday Book concentrated on getting information from reeves.

A volume of the Domesday Book.

- William I died on 9 September 1087, having defeated the Saxon English, built castles across England and established control of the country.

> **Quick Test**

1. Where did rebellions take place against Norman rule?
2. Who led a Saxon rebellion for over a decade?
3. What was the small hill called on which Normans built their castles?
4. What was the name of the book that contained William's survey of England?
5. In what year did William die?

> **Timeline**

1066 Battle of Hastings; William is crowned king.
1066–76 Rebellion of Hereward the Wake.
1069 Rebellion against William I in northern England.
1085–86 Domesday Book compiled.
1087 William I dies.

Christendom and the Crusades 1

You must be able to:

- Describe how religion was organised in the Middle Ages
- Explain why religion was important to people
- Explain why the Church was so powerful.

Why was Religion so Important in the Middle Ages?

- In the Middle Ages, religion was the most important thing in most people's lives.
- The vast majority of people were illiterate and looked to religion as a way to organise their lives.
- The fear of death was felt by everyone in a time when there was only basic medical knowledge and for most people life was nasty, brutish and short.
- Virtually everyone in England at this time were Christians.
- There was also a very small population of Jews.
- Christianity was divided into two parts:
  - In Western Europe the Christian Church looked to the Pope in Rome as leader.
  - In Eastern Europe people followed Orthodox Christianity and looked to the Emperor of Byzantium as leader.
- The whole area under Christian rule was called Christendom.

Organisation of the Churches and Monasteries

- In England the head of the country was the King, supported by barons and knights.
- There was a separate organisation for the Christian Church.
- The Head of the Western Church was the Pope, in Rome, Italy.
- The Pope was chosen by senior churchmen called cardinals.
- In England the most senior churchman was the Archbishop of Canterbury.
- Below him were bishops who organised the Church across England in areas known as dioceses.
- Within each diocese were hundreds of parishes, each led by a parish priest who performed religious services in a church.
- There were also monasteries and convents where religious people worked and prayed. These were led by abbots and abbesses.
- These looked after monks, nuns and friars, who were religious people who chose to live in monasteries and convents to pray and to do good works.

> ### Key Point
>
> Byzantium was a Christian empire in Eastern Europe centred on Constantinople, now known as Istanbul. It covered the area east of Italy and south of Ukraine.

> ### Key Point
>
> Monasteries were religious houses for men and convents were religious houses for women.

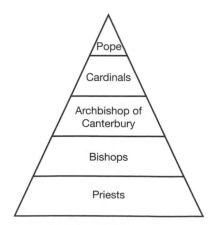

Organisation of the Church.

Why was the Christian Church so Powerful?

- The Christian Church owned large amounts of land making it rich and powerful.
- Monasteries and churches employed thousands of people to help the bishops, priests and monks.
- Life was unpredictable, with a constant fear of disease and death, but many believed that the Church offered a route to everlasting life in heaven.
- Even the King and lords looked to the Church to help them get to heaven.
- One of the Pope's greatest powers was his ability to excommunicate people, even kings.
- Excommunicants were no longer members of the Church, and it was believed that when they died they would go to hell, a place ruled by the Devil.
- Many believed that people in hell would face everlasting punishment and pain.
- Many English kings and lords at this time were illiterate (unable to read), like the vast majority of the population.
- The Church was home to priests and monks who could read and write. They were employed by the King and lords to help them administer their lands.
- One of the only ways ordinary people could leave their town or village would be by going on a pilgrimage.
- A pilgrimage is a journey to a religious place, usually associated with a holy person whose remains or relics could be seen.
- Pilgrimages were regarded as a help in the quest for heaven.

A stained glass window of a monk.

> ## Key Point
>
> Many beliefs held by Christians in the Middle Ages are still upheld by people today.

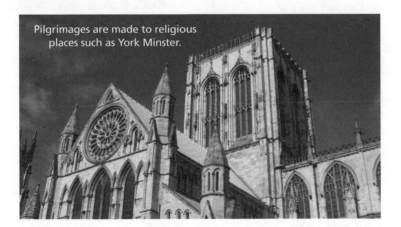

Pilgrimages are made to religious places such as York Minster.

> ## Quick Test
>
> 1. Who was head of the Western Christian Church?
> 2. Who was the most senior churchman in England?
> 3. Who lived and worked in monasteries and convents?
> 4. What did it mean to be excommunicated?
> 5. Why did people want to go on pilgrimages?

Christendom and the Crusades 2

You must be able to:

- Describe why Henry II and Thomas A'Becket quarrelled
- Explain why the Crusades took place
- Explain who won the Crusades.

The Struggle for Power Between the King and the Church

- The King and the Church usually worked well together.
- The Church enjoyed the protection of the King and gave its support to the King.
- The King enjoyed the support of the Church and the work of literate bishops and monks.
- In the late 12th century a conflict developed between King Henry II and the Archbishop of Canterbury, Thomas A'Becket.
- A'Becket had once been Henry's chief minister.
- When he became archbishop, A'Becket wanted the Church to be separate from the King, in particular in courts of law. A'Becket supported separate Church Courts for priests and monks. Henry wanted the clergy to be tried in the same courts as ordinary people to ensure fairness.
- In 1170, some knights murdered A'Becket in Canterbury Cathedral.
- They thought they were acting for the King, but there was outrage. Henry II felt very guilty and volunteered to be punished – he was flogged in public.
- A'Becket was made a saint, or holy man of the Church, and Canterbury became a place of pilgrimage.

Why did the Crusades Take Place?

- The Crusades were a series of wars between Christians and Muslims over control of the Holy Land, modern-day Israel.
- The main goal of the Crusades was to capture Jerusalem, the city where Jesus was crucified.
- The Crusades began in the late 11th century and lasted hundreds of years.
- The Pope hoped the Crusades would make the Church even more powerful.
- People went on Crusades for many reasons:
  - Some kings and lords were seeking money and power.
  - Others believed it would get them into heaven when they died.
  - Criminals and thieves went to escape punishment.

Key Point

As priests and monks made up the vast majority of those who were literate (able to read and write) this gave the Church much power.

In 1170 Thomas A'Becket was killed in Canterbury Cathedral.

Key Point

After death, Christians believe good people go to heaven, where they achieve everlasting happiness. The opposite of heaven is hell.

Who Won the Crusades?

- In 1099, the Crusaders captured Jerusalem and created a Christian kingdom in the Holy Land.
- Within 100 years Muslims had recaptured most of the Holy Land.
- Salah u Din, known as Saladin, was a major Muslim warrior king who controlled the Holy Land between 1174 and 1193.
- In 1187, he won a great victory over the Crusaders at the Battle of Hattin.
- One of Saladin's main Christian opponents was the English King Richard I, who was known as Richard the Lionheart.
- He fought Saladin in the Third Crusade but failed to capture Jerusalem.
- In 1212, there was even a Children's Crusade when 30 000 children from France and Germany tried to reach Jerusalem.
- Many of the children were sold into slavery by fellow Christians.
- Although the Crusaders had some success and ruled the Holy Land for part of the Middle Ages, for most of the time the area was controlled by Muslims.

Saladin.

Key Point

Jerusalem is a holy city for Christians, Muslims and Jews.

Crusaders and Muslims at war.

Quick Test

1. Which archbishop did Henry II quarrel with?
2. When was the archbishop killed?
3. Why might a criminal go on a Crusade?
4. Who was Saladin?
5. Who was known as the Lionheart?

Timeline

1096–99 The First Crusade.
1147–49 The Second Crusade.
1170 Archbishop Thomas A'Becket murdered in Canterbury.
1187 Battle of Hattin.
1189–92 The Third Crusade.
1202–04 The Fourth Crusade.
1212 The Children's Crusade.

Magna Carta 1

You must be able to:

- Describe the problems facing King John
- Explain why John had problems with the barons and the Church
- Explain what Magna Carta was.

What Problems did King John Face?

- King John replaced his brother Richard I, known as the Lionheart, in 1199 after Richard was killed in France.
- Richard I had left England in a great deal of debt due to wars with France and the Third Crusade.

Statue of Richard the Lionheart, outside the Houses of Parliament in London.

- Richard I had been a great warrior king while John was regarded as weak. His nickname was 'John soft sword'.
- When he became King of England, John had problems controlling his lands in Wales and Ireland.
- John also faced attacks from Scotland, which was an independent country.
- During most of his reign England was at war with France.
- By 1204, John had lost most of England's territories in France, such as Normandy.

Key Point

When John became King, England also ruled Wales, most of Ireland and a large part of northern France.

Problems with the Church

- In 1205, the Pope appointed Stephen Langton as Archbishop of Canterbury, the most senior position in the English Church.
- John disliked Stephen Langton and wanted his own choice of archbishop.
- In 1205, the Pope, Innocent III, stopped all religious ceremonies such as marriages and burials in England. This lasted for seven years.
- John, in return, took money from the Church and expelled monks from England.
- In 1209, the Pope excommunicated John, which meant John was no longer a member of Church.
- This quarrel seriously weakened John's position as king.

King John.

Problems with the Barons

- Barons were the most powerful people in England, after the King.
- They owned most of the land and provided most of King John's army.
- Barons expected their king to be a good warrior and to involve them in running the country.
- John was a poor warrior who tried to rule on his own.
- He also gave top jobs in his government to foreigners rather than barons.
- John's wars with France, Scotland, Wales and Ireland were very costly and the King expected the barons to pay extra taxes to fund them.

Was King John a bad king?

- Some historians would argue that King John was not as bad as people have made out.
- John was a very good organiser and manager.
- He was very intelligent and good at planning military tactics.

What was Magna Carta?

- Magna Carta was a charter signed in 1215 at Runnymede, an island in the River Thames, west of London.
- Magna Carta is Latin for 'Great Charter'. Latin was the language used in government in England at the time.
- The charter was an agreement between King John and the most senior landowners in England, the barons.
- The agreement limited the powers of the English King and protected the rights of the barons.
- It also gave Englishmen certain important civil rights such as trial by a jury of fellow Englishmen.
- It is regarded as one of the most important documents in English history and helped lead to the creation of the national parliament we have today.

Magna Carta Memorial, Runnymede.

Quick Test

1. What was John's nickname?
2. What was the name of the Archbishop of Canterbury appointed by the Pope in 1205?
3. What actions did the Pope take against King John?
4. How did King John try to punish the Church?
5. What does Magna Carta mean in English?

Magna Carta 2

You must be able to:

- Explain why King John agreed to Magna Carta
- Describe the changes made by Magna Carta
- Explain the importance of Magna Carta in English history.

Why King John Signed Magna Carta

- By 1214, John had fought wars with France, Wales, Ireland and Scotland.
- In 1214, he lost Poitou, an area of France that had been controlled by England.
- For five years, churches were closed on the orders of the Pope. People were worried that they would go to hell as a result.
- In 1214, King John went to war against the barons.
- The extra taxes that John demanded had forced the barons to rebel and form their own army.
- In May 1215, the barons captured London.
- In June, the barons forced King John to sign an agreement at Runnymede, near Windsor, west of London.
- This was Magna Carta, or Great Charter.
- King John hoped that signing Magna Carta would stop the barons' rebellion.

> ### Key Point
>
> By 1215, John had fallen out with the barons and the Church and had been defeated in war by France.

What Changes did Magna Carta Make?

- Magna Carta made changes to King John's relations with the Church, the barons and ordinary people.
- The first part of Magna Carta stated that the King would not interfere with the Church.
- The next part stated that when a baron inherited land he should not pay more than £100 to the King.
- Another important part said that the King could not raise any new taxes without the agreement of the barons and bishops.
- Freemen could not be put in prison without a trial by a jury of freemen.
- The King's judges had to be fair to everyone.
- Everyone was free to enter or leave England. They did not need the King's permission.

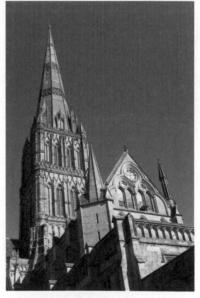

A copy of Magna Carta is kept in Salisbury Cathedral.

The Importance of Magna Carta

- Magna Carta was the first time an English King had agreed to protect the rights of Englishmen in writing.
- It was important because the King no longer ruled without the support of the barons and the Church.
- It gave freemen (people who are not villeins) in England certain rights.
- Magna Carta protected the rights of the rich and powerful barons and the Church.
- Most Englishmen were not freemen but villeins, so were unaffected by Magna Carta.

The Creation of Parliament

- If a king wanted to raise taxes he had to consult his Great Council, made up of barons and bishops.
- Under John's son, King Henry III, England's first Parliament was called in 1265 by Simon de Montfort.
- This Parliament contained barons, bishops, two knights from each county and town representatives.
- Barons and bishops formed the House of Lords.
- Knights and townspeople formed the House of Commons. The members of the House of Commons were elected.
- These changes laid the foundations of the Houses of Parliament we have today.

The Houses of Parliament today.

> ## Key Point
>
> Parliament replaced the Great Council as the main voice of the rich and powerful of England. Its support became important for future kings to raise taxation.

> ## Timeline
>
> **1199** John becomes King.
> **1204** King John loses Normandy to France.
> **1205** John has a major argument with the Pope.
> **1209** The Pope excommunicates John.
> **1214** War breaks out between John and the barons.
> **1215** John signs Magna Carta.
> **1265** England's first Parliament meets.

> ## Quick Test
>
> 1. In what year did the barons capture London?
> 2. Where was Magna Carta signed?
> 3. After Magna Carta was introduced, what was the maximum amount a baron had to pay the King when he inherited land?
> 4. Who formed the House of Lords?
> 5. Who formed the House of Commons?

The Black Death 1

You must be able to:

- Explain the real cause of the Black Death
- Describe how people died of the Black Death
- Explain what people at the time thought caused the Black Death.

What was the Black Death?

- The Black Death was a severe outbreak of disease that affected England from 1348 to 1350.
- It was bubonic plague and was spread by fleas carried by black rats.
- The disease orginated in the Middle East and was brought to England by black rats on boats from Europe.
- It spread from ports all over the country within a year and had a devastating effect on England.
- The Black Death killed about one-third of the population – 1.5 million people died out of a population of 4 million.
- About 200 million people died in Europe.
- In China the population dropped from 125 million to just 90 million in 50 years because of the Black Death.
- In England, 7 500 people a day died of the Black Death.
- Everyone was affected – old and young, rich and poor.
- Even King Edward III's daughter, Joan, died of the disease.

Beliefs about the Black Death

- Although the Black Death was brought to England by rats on ships, it was the fleas that lived on the rats that caused the disease.
- In the Middle Ages, people lived in primitive conditions and had very poor hygiene.
- Modern-day toilets and waste disposal did not exist. Sewage flowed in the streets, which led to the rapid spread of disease.
- Although doctors now know how the disease spread, in 1348 the vast majority of people were illiterate and very little was known about the causes of disease.
- Many people thought the disease was a punishment from God and therefore felt that if they prayed a lot it would save them. Others whipped themselves as a form of punishment to please God.

Key Point

The bubonic plague caused the Black Death. People who caught the disease suffered severe flu symptoms, coughing, and swollen lumps on the arms and legs.

The Black Death was spread by fleas on black rats.

The Black Death was spread by fleas.

- A popular idea was that the end of the world was coming. Venus, Mars and Jupiter were all seen together in the sky in 1348, making people think a disaster was going to happen.
- A popular belief was that the disease was spread by 'bad air'.
- One method of dealing with the disease was to seal victims near a large fire, which would destroy the bad air.
- Other people, including plague doctors, placed sweet-smelling dried flowers and herbs over their nose and mouth to prevent the bad air from entering their body.
- Others used dried toads and leeches as a way of removing the poison from diseased bodies.
- People put figs and butter on the swollen lumps to soften them.

Key Point

Doctors were unable to prevent or cure the Black Death.

Figs were placed on swollen lumps.

Butter was used to soften the swollen lumps.

Treating a sufferer of the Black Death.

Quick Test

1. When was the first outbreak of the Black Death?
2. Where did the Black Death originate?
3. How did people get the disease?
4. How many people died of the Black Death in Europe?
5. Which animals did people use to treat the Black Death?

The Black Death 2

You must be able to:

- Describe the symptoms of the Black Death
- Explain the immediate impact of the Black Death
- Explain how the Black Death affected England in the following 100 years.

Symptoms of the Black Death

- People learnt to identify the symptoms of the Black Death through observation.
- To begin with victims suffered from flu symptoms of sweating and coughing.
- Then large lumps appeared on their bodies, usually on the arms and legs.
- These lumps, or buboes, were first red in colour, full of blood, but then turned black, giving the disease its name. Lumps went black as blood in the body dried out.
- Victims suffered high temperatures.
- Blotches appeared all over the body.
- Most people who caught the Black Death died within five days.

Social Effects of the Black Death

- Whole villages and towns were wiped out by the Black Death.
- The population of England dropped by about one-third in two years because of the disease.
- People began leaving towns and going to live in the countryside in an attempt to avoid it.
- Foreigners and non-Christians, such as Jews, were attacked because some people blamed them for causing the disease.
- Jews were forced to live in separate parts of towns and others were banned altogether.

Economic Effects of the Black Death

- With fewer peasants much agricultural land was unused.
- Peasants left their fields and unattended livestock were left to die.
- Food supplies started to run low and prices rose.
- As there were fewer peasants to work the land and fewer craftsmen in towns these people began to demand higher wages.

> **Key Point**
>
> The loss of one-third of the population saw hundreds of villages abandoned. New towns developed as people moved to different areas.

Livestock died as a result of fewer peasants to take care of them.

- Villeins began to refuse to work on the lord's land for free. They disliked this obligation and resented having to pay taxes.
- Lords offered villeins more food and money to work their land, so those who survived benefited from the changes brought by the Black Death.

The Next 100 Years

- Over the 50 years after the Black Death many villages were abandoned as their populations dropped so severely that village life could not survive.
- Hundreds of villages disappeared. Several of these lost villages were rediscovered in the 20th century through aerial photography.
- Many people began to lose faith in the Christian Church.
- They had been told that the Black Death was a punishment from God but churchmen and those who prayed also died.
- There were fewer people to provide religious help as 40 per cent of priests and monks had died in the Black Death.
- In 1349 a law was passed, the Ordinance of Labourers, that tried to keep wages at pre-Black Death levels, but it was ignored.
- The loss of population led to the need for more machines to help produce goods such as cloth.
- When the Poll Tax was introduced in 1381, 30 years after the Black Death, a major rebellion took place called the Peasants' Revolt.

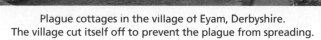

Plague cottages in the village of Eyam, Derbyshire. The village cut itself off to prevent the plague from spreading.

> ### Key Point
>
> The Black Death returned roughly every 10 years and the population of England declined over the following 100 years.

> ### Timeline
>
> **June 1348** Black Death arrives in England at Melcombe Regis (Weymouth) in Dorset.
> **Aug 1348** Black Death hits Bristol.
> **Sept 1348** Black Death reaches London.
> **Jan 1349** Parliament stopped meeting because of the plague.
> **Jan–Feb 1349** Black Death spreads into East Anglia and the Midlands.
> **April 1349** Black Death reported in Wales.
> **July 1349** Black Death hits Ireland.

> ### Quick Test
>
> 1. What were the symptoms of the Black Death?
> 2. How long did people who caught the Black Death normally survive?
> 3. Which group of people were blamed and forced to live in separate parts of town?
> 4. How did the Black Death affect food prices?
> 5. How were the surviving villeins affected after the Black Death?

Review Questions

KS2 Key Concepts

1 Place the following events in the correct chronological order.

    a) The Roman invasion of Britain by Claudius.

    b) Augustine's mission sets up Christianity in Britain.

    c) Iron Age hill forts are built in Britain.

    d) Alfred the Great rules England.

    e) Boudicca's uprising against the Romans.   [5]

2 Fill in the blanks in the sentences using the words below.

Lindisfarne	**Anglo-Saxon**	**Roman**	**St Cuthbert**	**Before**

Julius Caesar was a _____ general. He invaded Britain in 55 BCE, which stands for _____ the Common Era.

Alfred the Great was an _____ king. He created peace between the Vikings and the English.

_____ was a Christian monk. He brought Christianity to northern England.

He built a big monastery on an island off the east coast of northern England called _____   [5]

3 Look back at question 2. Who do you think was **most** important out of Julius Caesar, Alfred the Great and St Cuthbert? Make sure you give a reason for your answer.   [2]

4 Look back at question 2. Who do you think was **least** important out of Julius Caesar, Alfred the Great and St Cuthbert? Make sure you give a reason for your answer.   [2]

5 Read the sources below then answer the questions.

> ***Source A: A modern historian's view***
>
> In today's society, nobody would be allowed to work in such awful conditions. Injuries such as the loss of fingers and hands, beatings from factory owners, and death were common. It is shocking that children were allowed to work in this type of setting.

Source B: Part of a factory owner's account after the passing of the Factory Act in 1833, which improved conditions for workers.

Working in factories is very beneficial for children. They are provided with food and water; they cannot work more than 48 hours per week and any child under the age of eleven receives two hours of schooling per day.

a) Using Source A, describe what conditions were like in factories during the Victorian period. [3]

b) Compare Sources A and B. How are they different? Give an example from both sources. [4]

c) Look at the origin of Source B (who wrote it). Why do you think the factory owner would want to show that conditions weren't as bad as people thought? [3]

6 In 1939, just under 1 million children from English cities such as London and Manchester were evacuated to the countryside for safety. Look at the photograph below then answer the questions.

a) How can you tell that these children are evacuees? [2]

b) Give examples of two effects that evacuation might have on:

    i) mothers who are sending their children away

    ii) children who are being sent away (evacuees)

    iii) the areas the evacuees have been sent away from. [6]

The Norman Conquest

1 Which country did the Saxons come from before they came to England?

_____ [1]

2 Which part of France was William the Conqueror originally from?

_____ [1]

3 Who led the Danes in the fight against the Saxons at Stamford Bridge?

_____ [1]

4 What was a 'bailey'?

_____ [1]

5 Why could William lay claim to the English throne?

In your answer you should:
- Give your opinion of William's three most important claims.
- Provide any other reason(s) William had a claim.
- Support your answer with facts and figures.

Write your answer on a separate sheet of paper. [10]

6 Why do you think William won the Battle of Hastings?

In your answer you should:
- Say why the Normans were in a better position than the Saxons.
- State some of the problems the Saxons faced.
- Use your own knowledge to support your answer.

Write your answer on a separate sheet of paper. [10]

Christendom and the Crusades

1 Who led the Orthodox Christians in the East of Europe?

.... [1]

2 What town became a place of pilgrimage following Thomas A'Becket's death?

.... [1]

3 What city in the Middle East were the Crusaders trying to capture?

.... [1]

4 What was a pilgrimage?

.... [1]

5 Imagine you are a villein in the Middle Ages. Explain why religion is important to you.

In your answer you should:
- Describe your life and what you do.
- Give at least two reasons why religion is important in your life.

Write your answer on a separate sheet of paper. [10]

6 In the Middle Ages, in what ways were the lives of priests and monks different?

In your answer you should:
- Give descriptions, in turn, of what priests and monks did in the Middle Ages.
- Use your own knowledge and evidence to explain how the lives of priests and monks were different.

Write your answer on a separate sheet of paper. [10]

Practice Questions

Magna Carta

1 When was Magna Carta signed?

.... [1]

2 What did Magna Carta limit?

.... [1]

3 What important civil right did Magna Carta give Englishmen?

.... [1]

4 What did the Pope do to King John in 1209?

.... [1]

5 Why have people seen King John as a weak king?

In your answer you should:
- Give your opinion, backed up with facts and figures.
- Explain why people, at the time and since, have thought John was weak.

Write your answer on a separate sheet of paper. [10]

6 Why do you think the barons had a quarrel with King John?

In your answer you should:
- Give at least three reasons, supported with facts and figures.
- Explain why these reasons caused the quarrel.
- Write at least two paragraphs: the first dealing with reasons caused by King John, and the second dealing with reasons caused by others.

Write your answer on a separate sheet of paper. [10]

The Black Death

1 How many people died each day of the Black Death in England?

.... [1]

2 What gave the disease its name?

.... [1]

3 How often did the Black Death reoccur in the 100 years after 1350?

.... [1]

4 How did villeins benefit from the Black Death?

.... [1]

5 Why were the symptoms of the Black Death so unpleasant?

In your answer you should:
- Give your opinion of why the symptoms were so unpleasant.
- Describe two of the worst symptoms.

Write your answer on a separate sheet of paper. [10]

6 How did people try to stop the spread of the Black Death in England?

In your answer you should:
- Give your opinion of how each method was intended to stop the spread of the disease.
- Write two paragraphs: the first dealing with religious ideas about the spread of the disease, and the second dealing with non-religious ideas.

Write your answer on a separate sheet of paper. [10]

The Peasants' Revolt 1

You must be able to:

- Describe the problems facing Richard II
- Explain how the war with France affected England
- Give reasons why the revolt took place.

England under Richard II

- Richard II became King in 1377 after the death of his grandfather, Edward III.
- He was only 10 years old in 1377 so England was ruled by his advisers.
- Unfortunately, this group of advisers did not include England's most important lord, John of Gaunt.
- Following the Black Death, when one-third of the population died, England was short of wealth.
- England ruled a large part of France, Wales and Ireland.
- Richard had inherited a very costly war against the French.
- The Hundred Years War against France was becoming more expensive to fight each year.

Key Point

When Richard II became King he was too young to rule on his own. A council of senior advisers was created that made all major decisions.

What was the Peasants' Revolt of 1381?

- The Peasants' Revolt in 1381 was the most serious rebellion in the Middle Ages.
- There were many reasons for the revolt including the introduction of Poll Tax and peasants wanting fairer rights.
- It started in Fobbing in Essex, and was centred on counties close to London, most notably Essex and Kent.

Areas affected by the Peasants' Revolt.

- The rebels entered London and came very close to overthrowing the government.
- The defeat of the Peasants' Revolt saved the reign of young King Richard II.
- To end the revolt Richard made many promises to the rebels, which he subsequently failed to keep.
- Although the King and lords triumphed, the shortage of labour after the Black Death meant that peasants' wages actually rose.

Causes of the Peasants' Revolt

- There were many causes of the Peasants' Revolt in 1381.
- The immediate cause of the revolt was the introduction of Poll Tax in 1380.
- Poll Tax was a tax paid by all adult men.
  - The tax was needed to pay for the ongoing war against France (the Hundred Years War).
  - Everyone, rich and poor, was charged the same amount of tax: five pence per person in England.
  - Peasants feared new taxes after the introduction of Poll Tax. There had already been tax rises in 1377, 1379 and 1380.
- After the Black Death there was a shortage of peasants and this led to their demands for wages.
  - At this time, peasants still worked for lords for no pay.
  - Many peasants had to work for free on Church land, sometimes for up to two days a week.
  - This meant that they could not work their own land, which made it difficult to feed their families.
  - Peasants wanted to be free of this burden, which made the Church rich at their expense.
- John Ball, a priest from Kent, said that God had not created rich and poor. Everyone should be seen as equal.
- Richard II was only 14 years old so the peasants believed he had been given poor advice by the Chancellor, Simon of Sudbury, and the Royal Treasurer, Sir Robert Hales.
- The rebellion was more against Richard II's advisers than the young king.

> **Key Point**
>
> The Hundred Years War between England and France was the longest war in history. It actually lasted 116 years, and ended with English defeat in 1453.

Richard II.

> **Quick Test**
>
> 1. What was the immediate cause of the Peasants' Revolt?
> 2. Which areas were at the centre of the rebellion?
> 3. How old was Richard II when he became King?
> 4. How much was the Poll Tax?
> 5. What was the name of the village in Essex where the rebellion began?

The Peasants' Revolt 2

You must be able to:

- Describe the main events of the Peasants' Revolt
- Explain how Richard II brought the revolt to an end
- Explain the effects of the revolt on England.

Main Events of the Revolt

- In May 1381, a tax collector arrived in the Essex village of Fobbing to find out why people had not paid the Poll Tax. He was thrown out by the villagers.
- In the same month, in Kent, some peasants seized a castle. They recognised Wat Tyler as their leader, the man who was to become head of the revolt.
- Soldiers were then sent to Fobbing in June.
- In response, the Fobbing peasants organised themselves into armed groups, which were supported by other Essex villages.
- This started an armed rebellion across Essex, which also spread to Kent.
- On 11 June, Kentish peasants marched on Blackheath, only five miles from London.
  - At the same time, Essex peasants marched on Mile End, just a few miles east of London.
  - In total, there were between 50 000 and 60 000 peasants involved in the revolt.
  - There were also peasant riots in Sussex, Surrey and as far away as Dorset.
- On 12 June, Richard II tried to speak to the peasants, but he failed to deter them.
- On 13 June, the rebels entered London and attacked the homes of the King's advisers.
- On 14 June, Richard II met the Essex rebels at Mile End.
  - Richard II promised to free any rebels from prison, pardon them and punish his advisers.
  - Some rebels murdered the Bishop of London and the Royal Treasurer.
  - They also murdered John Legge, the organiser of the Poll Tax.
- On 15 June, Wat Tyler met Richard II.
  - Tyler demanded that all men should be free and that the Church's wealth should be given to the poor.
  - Tyler was killed by the Mayor of London, William Walworth, after an argument.

Key Point

Peasants were agricultural labourers, most of whom were villeins. As England was mainly an agricultural country they produced most of the country's wealth.

Wat Tyler killing a tax collector.

William Walworth kills Wat Tyler.

- Richard II agreed to all the rebels' demands. They returned to their homes thinking they had won.
- Apart from putting an end to the Poll Tax, Richard II went on to break all the promises he had made.

Reasons for the Revolt's Failure

- There were several reasons for the failure of the Peasants' Revolt:
  - The rebels lacked discipline and organisation.
  - Most of the rebels accepted Richard II's promises and therefore returned home.
  - Richard had John Ball and many rebel leaders hanged.
  - In Essex and Kent, 8000 royal troops restored order, killing 1500 rebels.
  - The King claimed all his promises were made under threat, so did not count.
  - The rebellion was based mainly in Essex and Kent, not across the whole country.

How Much did England Change After the Peasants' Revolt?

- Although the Peasants' Revolt failed, it did have an impact on the future of life in England.
- The Poll Tax was withdrawn. When it was reintroduced in the late 1980s it caused riots in London in 1990.
- The shortage of labour caused by the Black Death eventually forced lords to pay peasants wages.
- Peasants' living standards rose over the following hundred years.
- The feudal system, which had been introduced by the Normans, began to collapse.
- Richard II, although only 14 years of age, showed great calm during the revolt and won admiration.
- His use of Parliament to raise money saved his rule for a while.
- In 1399, however, he was murdered and replaced by Henry IV.
- By 1500, there were no longer any villeins. All Englishmen were freemen and benefited from the rights in Magna Carta.

Quick Test

1. Who was the leader of the Peasants' Revolt?
2. Where did Richard meet the rebels?
3. What did Richard promise the rebels, which ended the revolt?
4. What was the only promise Richard kept?
5. What happened when the Poll Tax reappeared in the 1980s?

Key Point

The feudal system was a way of organising society introduced in England after 1066. The King granted land to lords and the Church in return for service. In turn, the local lord or the Church gave peasants land for which they had to work several days a week for free as villeins.

The reintroduction of a poll tax caused riots in London in 1990.

Timeline

1377 Richard II becomes King at the age of ten.
1380 Poll Tax is introduced.
May–June 1381 Peasants' Revolt breaks out in Essex and Kent.
1381 Poll Tax is withdrawn.
1500 The feudal system ends; all Englishmen are freemen.

Reformation and Counter-Reformation 1

You must be able to:

- Explain why the Reformation took place under Henry VIII
- Describe the main changes made under Henry VIII
- Explain how far England had become a Protestant country by 1547.

What were the Reformation and Counter-Reformation?

- In the first half of the 16th century, Europe saw a major split in the Christian Church.
- People began to question the authority of the Pope and the Catholic Church.
- At this time the Bible, Christianity's holy book, was only available in Latin, but many people wanted to read it in their own language.
- Others wanted to run their own church services.
- These changes first began in Germany, and came to be called the Reformation.
- Those who opposed the Pope and the Catholic Church were known as Protestants.
- The Catholic Church responded by reforming itself and trying to win back lands that had become Protestant. This was called the Counter-Reformation.

> ### Key Point
>
> Catholic refers to the parts of the Western Christian Church that stayed loyal to the Pope. Protestant refers to those areas of Europe that rejected the Pope's authority and wanted new ways of organising the Christian religion.

Henry VIII's Break with Rome

- One of Henry's biggest aims was to have a son who would follow him as king.
- Unfortunately his wife, Catherine of Aragon, produced only a daughter, Mary (later to become Mary I).
- Henry decided to divorce Catherine, who was too old to have any more children, but he needed the support of the Pope to do so.
- The Pope, Clement VII, refused as he was a prisoner of Catherine's nephew, the Holy Roman Emperor Charles V.
- Henry VIII divorced Catherine and married Anne Boleyn in the hope of having a son. She had a daughter, Elizabeth (later to become Elizabeth I).
- He persuaded Parliament to pass the Act of Supremacy in 1534. This made Henry VIII 'Supreme Head of the Church' in place of the Pope.

Henry VIII.

Dissolving the Monasteries

- Henry VIII feared that monastic communities still supported the Pope, even though he had made himself Head of the Church.
- He also wanted the lands and wealth of the monasteries to build up his armed forces.
- Henry ordered a survey to find out how much wealth the monasteries possessed and to show that monks and nuns were not living religious lives.
- In 1536, Henry VIII decided to dissolve (close) the monasteries.
- By 1540, over 800 monasteries had been closed and their wealth taken by Henry and his supporters.
- Opposition to Henry's actions led to a rebellion in 1536 in northern England called the Pilgrimage of Grace.
- Henry defeated the rebellion and executed its leaders, including Robert Aske.

The ruins of Kirkstall Abbey, Leeds, which was dissolved by Henry VIII.

> **Key Point**
>
> Before the Reformation the Pope chose the Archbishop of Canterbury, bishops and abbots of monasteries. Large sums of money were also sent from England to Rome to fund the Pope and Church government. All this stopped in the Reformation.

The Church under Henry VIII

- Henry changed the way the Church worked.
- He appointed the Archbishop of Canterbury and all the bishops, instead of the Pope.
- All churches were ordered to have a Bible in English for people to read.
- Church services were in English rather than Latin.
- England no longer looked to the Pope for guidance and stopped sending him money.

> **Quick Test**
>
> 1. Before the Reformation, what was the only language in which the Bible was available?
> 2. In what country did the Reformation begin?
> 3. Why did Henry VIII divorce Catherine of Aragon?
> 4. Who did he marry next?
> 5. In what year did Henry begin dissolving the monasteries?

Reformation and Counter-Reformation 2

You must be able to:

- Explain the religious changes under Edward VI
- Describe the Counter Reformation under Mary I.

The Six Articles

- The Church in England was now separate from most of the Christian Church in Europe.
- In 1539 Henry VIII published the Six Articles.
- These set out the religious beliefs of the Church in England and were very similar to those of the Catholic Church.
- Anyone not following the Six Articles faced death. Between 1539 and his death in 1547 Henry executed thousands of Protestants for not following his Six Articles of religious faith.

Edward VI makes England a Protestant Country

- Henry VIII eventually had a son, Edward (later to become Edward VI), with his third wife Jane Seymour.
- When Henry VIII died, Edward VI became king, but he was only nine years old.
- His advisers, most importantly Edward Seymour, Duke of Somerset, decided to make England a more Protestant country.
- In 1549 Edward allowed priests in the Church in England to marry. Catholic priests were forbidden from doing so.
- Priests were no longer expected to wear elaborate robes but simple clothing.
- Edward also introduced a new Book of Common Prayer, written by Archbishop of Canterbury, Thomas Cranmer.
- The new Book of Common Prayer was written in English and contained new religious services.
- The main Catholic service, the Mass, was abolished. It was replaced by a simple Holy Communion where bread and wine were shared.
- Religious statues and paintings were removed from churches and church walls were whitewashed.
- The Catholic altar was replaced by a simple table as the centre of religious services.
- Edward also closed all remaining monasteries.

Key Point

Catholics believe that in the main part of their religious service, the Mass, the bread and wine offered by a priest actually became the body and blood of Jesus. Protestants believed that their service was simple and symbolic and they rejected the Catholic view.

Thomas Cranmer wrote the new Book of Common Prayer in English.

The Counter-Reformation under Mary I

- When Edward VI died at the age of 15, he was succeeded by his older sister Mary I, who had been brought up as a Catholic.
- Mary was determined to bring back the Catholic religion.
- She married Philip of Spain, one of Europe's most important Catholic monarchs.
- She recognised the Pope as Head of the Church in England.
- Protestant bishops and priests were removed and replaced by Catholic ones.
- The Mass returned as the main religious service.
- Many opponents of these Catholic changes were put to death.
- Over 200 Protestants were burnt at the stake, giving Mary I the nickname 'Bloody Mary'.
- Mary I's reign was as short as her brother's. She died in 1558 without a child.
- Mary I was succeed by her younger sister, Elizabeth I, who had been brought up as a Protestant.
- In 1559, Elizabeth I returned England to being a Protestant country.
- The Counter-Reformation had been shortlived. Since 1558, England has officially been a Protestant country with the monarch as Head of the Church of England.

Key Point

The Counter Reformation took place across Europe. Catholic countries like Spain executed Protestants and sought to destroy Protestantism wherever it existed.

Mary I.

Elizabeth I.

Timeline

1509 Henry VIII becomes King.
1533 Henry divorces Catherine of Aragon.
1534 Henry VIII makes himself Supreme Head of the Church in England.
1536 Henry begins closing monasteries.
1547 Edward VI makes England a Protestant country.
1553 Mary I becomes Queen and the Counter Reformation begins.
1558 Mary I dies and is replaced by the Protestant Elizabeth I.

Quick Test

1. In what year were the Six Articles published?
2. Who was Edward VI's chief adviser?
3. In which language was the Book of Common Prayer written?
4. How did the Protestant religious service differ from the Catholic Mass?
5. Why was Mary I nicknamed 'Bloody Mary'?

The English Civil War 1

You must be able to:

- Explain the causes of the war
- Understand who fought on each side
- Understand the significance of the Battle of Edgehill and the Battle of Marston Moor.

What Caused the English Civil War?

- Charles I became King in 1625.
- There were many causes of the English Civil War between 1642 and 1648.

Religion

- Charles I was married to a French Roman Catholic, Henrietta Maria.
- William Laud, one of Charles's advisers, introduced unpopular ideas such as burning incense and candles during church services. These were seen as Catholic practices at a time when England was Protestant.
- In 1637, Charles tried to enforce a new prayer book in Scotland.
- Most Members of Parliament were Puritan (strict Protestants), and disapproved of Charles's Catholic connections.

Power

- Charles was often seen as arrogant. He strongly believed in the 'Divine Right of Kings', which meant God had chosen him to be King and no one could question that choice.
- Charles ruled without Parliament between 1629 and 1640. This is known as the 'eleven years of tyranny'.
- Charles used the private Court of the Star Chamber to ruthlessly punish his opponents, and fine people when he was short of money.
- In 1642, Charles attempted to arrest five Members of Parliament, including Oliver Cromwell, on a charge of treason when they refused to give in to his demands.

Money

- Charles was known for his extravagant, expensive lifestyle, which often left him needing more money.
- In 1635, he extended Ship Tax, previously only paid in coastal areas, to the whole country.
- He fought two expensive and unsuccessful wars, with Spain in 1625 and France in 1627.
- After the Scots rebelled in 1640, he was forced to ask Parliament for more money to be able to fight another war.

Key Point

Many of the causes of the civil wars were linked to more than one problem. For example, the problems with Scotland were linked to both religion and money.

Charles I.

A Country Divided

- The English Civil War was fought by the Royalists (Cavaliers) and Parliamentarians (Roundheads).
- The Cavaliers were:
  - supported by most of the gentry
  - often from northern and western regions, with some Irish, Scottish and Welsh soldiers
  - had the better horsemen, or cavalry, which is where they get their name Cavaliers
  - generally conservative Protestant or Catholic
  - mainly led by Charles's nephew, Prince Rupert.
- The Roundheads were:
  - mainly merchants and traders
  - generally from London and the south-east
  - in control of London and the navy, increasing their power
  - mainly Puritan, a strict Protestant movement
  - latterly led by Oliver Cromwell, who proved himself a key solider.

Battle of Edgehill, 23 October 1642

- War broke out in August 1642, but Edgehill was the first major battle.
- The two sides stumbled upon each other as Charles marched his army from Shrewsbury to London.
- There was a stalemate situation many times in the battle, with neither side advancing.
- Both sides lost approximately 1500 men, and both declared a victory although there was no clear winner.
- The Cavaliers had intended to continue the battle the following day, but decided against it as their troops were exhausted.

Battle of Marston Moor, 2 July 1644

- This important battle ended any significant Royalist support in the north.
- Prince Rupert had marched into York, a powerful city, quite easily.
- The Royalists' power over York gave them an advantage.
- The battle started to go wrong as the Royalist men arrived bit by bit.
- Their 18 000 men were soon outnumbered by 28 000 Roundheads, causing them to lose.

> **Key Point**
>
> Having his nephew lead his army, rather than doing it himself, did nothing to improve Charles I's popularity.

Prince Rupert.

Monument at the site of the Battle of Marston Moor.

Quick Test

1. Why was Charles I's wife unpopular?
2. What did Charles introduce that angered the Scots?
3. Who led King Charles's army?
4. What was the first major battle of the war?
5. At which battle did Charles lose control of the north of England?

The English Civil War 2

You must be able to:

- Understand the significance of the Battle of Naseby
- Know what is meant by the Second English Civil War
- Understand the uncertainty around Charles's trial and execution.

Battle of Naseby, 14 June 1645

- Charles's confidence had been boosted by a relatively easy attack on Leicester in May.
- He then decided to try to take Oxford, a key Parliamentarian stronghold.
- He started well but his commanders had become divided.
- Cromwell had developed a 'New Model Army', meaning soldiers were to be trained in peace time as well as war.
- Many of Charles's supporters were late as they were travelling from Wales and Somerset. Some never arrived.
- Charles was soon outnumbered by between 8 000 and 13 000 men.
- Many see Parliament's victory at Naseby as a turning point in the war.
- Following this battle, in September Prince Rupert surrendered Bristol to Parliament.
- Charles withdrew his position in the army, and Rupert fled to Holland.

Key Point

The establishment of the New Model Army prior to the Battle of Naseby was a key step in bringing Oliver Cromwell to prominence.

The Second English Civil War

- Following Naseby, there was a series of smaller defeats for the Royalists, but the war was all but over.
- In 1646, Charles gave himself up to the Scots, who eventually surrendered him to Parliament in January 1647.
- Charles fled from Hampton Court Palace, where he was being held, in November 1647.
- Ironically, Charles sided with the Scots, and raised another army, who invaded England. This is sometimes known as the Second English Civil War.
- There were a number of Royalist uprisings, but most were easily put down by the New Model Army.
- The Royalists lacked leadership, money and support. Charles was eventually recaptured in August 1648.

Hampton Court Palace.

The Trial of King Charles I

- There had been much discussion about what to do with the captured King.
- Many MPs did not want the King to stand trial.
- Cromwell only allowed MPs into Parliament if he believed they wanted the King to stand trial. This was known as the 'Rump Parliament'.
- However, only 29 of these 46 politicians voted for the King to stand trial.
- The trial started on 1 January 1649.
- Charles was the first monarch ever to be put on trial.
- He was accused of being a 'tyrant, traitor and murderer'.
- Of the 135 judges expected at the trial, only 68 attended.
- The chief judge was John Bradshaw, a lawyer, after no one else was willing to take the job.
- Charles refused to defend himself until after the judgment of the court was read.
- He was found guilty of all charges and sentenced to be executed on 30 January 1649.
- Cromwell's signature can be clearly seen on Charles's death warrant. He is widely rumoured to have been a key supporter in the decision to kill the King.

The Execution of Charles I

- Charles was executed on scaffolding erected outside the Banqueting Hall in London.
- His execution was delayed as the executioner scheduled to carry out the beheading refused to do it.
- It was a struggle to find anyone willing to kill the King.
- Eventually two executioners were paid highly to do the job, on the reassurance they could wear masks throughout so no one would know who they were.
- Charles allegedly wore two shirts as it was a cold day. He did not want to shiver and lead the crowd to believe he was afraid.
- Spectators dipped their handkerchiefs into his blood following the execution owing to the belief that the King's blood had healing powers.

Charles I on trial.

> **Key Point**
>
> An English monarch had never been executed before Charles I, so there was much uncertainty around his trial and execution.

> **Timeline**
>
> **August 1642** War breaks out.
> **October 1642** Battle of Edgehill.
> **July 1644** Battle of Marston Moor.
> **June 1645** Battle of Naseby.
> **January 1647** Charles is given to Parliament.
> **November 1647** Charles escapes.
> **August 1648** Charles is recaptured.
> **January 1649** Charles is executed.

Quick Test

1. What did Cromwell develop prior to the Battle of Naseby?
2. Which city did Prince Rupert surrender to Parliament?
3. Who did Charles side with after fleeing from Hampton Court Palace?
4. How did Cromwell select MPs for the Rump Parliament?
5. When was Charles's execution?

The Interregnum 1

You must be able to:

- Describe the events leading to Cromwell becoming Lord Protector
- Explain what the republic was
- Explain who the Puritans were.

What is the Interregnum?

- The Interregnum is the period of British history between 1649 and 1660 in which Oliver Cromwell ruled the country as Lord Protector.
- The period began with the execution of Charles I on 30 January 1649 and ended with the restoration of the monarchy by Charles II on 29 May 1660.

England Becomes a Republic

- Following the death of Charles I in January 1649, Parliament passed laws that abolished the monarchy, the House of Lords and the Church of England.
- Parliament declared that England should be a republic. This meant the country would be ruled without a king or queen.
- The most powerful person in the country was Oliver Cromwell.
- Cromwell and most of the army officers were Puritans.
- Parliament did not want to pass the laws that the army wanted, and this caused arguments and tension.
- On 20 April 1653, Cromwell and the army went to Parliament and expelled the MPs.

> ### Key Point
>
> The Puritans believed that God was on their side and that this was the reason for their victory in the Civil War. They believed that England should be a more religiously strict country.

The Barebones Parliament

- Oliver Cromwell selected 140 Puritans to become MPs in a new Parliament. This was named the Barebones Parliament after one of the leaders – Praise-God Barebones.
- Cromwell soon found that some of these new MPs had very extreme views, which he did not like. These included getting rid of tithes (a sort of tax) and changing the law so that theft was no longer punishable by death.
- A number of the moderate MPs voted to end Parliament.

The Instrument of Government

- A new Parliament with a new constitution, known as the Instrument of Government, was set up. It said that only godly and religious men could become Members of Parliament.
- Cromwell became head of the government for life, called Lord Protector.

Oliver Cromwell.

- Cromwell was now in charge of the country and still retained the support of a strong army.

The Council of State

- The Council of State had been appointed following the execution of the King in 1649. Its function was to implement domestic and foreign policy, and ensure the security of the country.
- The Council of State became an advisory service to Cromwell.
- Between 13 and 21 councillors were elected by Parliament to advise the Protector.
- In reality, Cromwell relied on the army for support and chose his own councillors.

The Houses of Parliament today.

Rule of the Major-Generals

- In spring 1655, Cromwell imposed direct military government in England and Wales.
- Cromwell divided England into military districts ruled by army Major-Generals who answered only to him.
- They were responsible for tax collection, local law enforcement, preventing opposition to Cromwell and imposing Cromwell's strict rules.
- This proved deeply unpopular and was seen as a military dictatorship.
- The rule of the Major-Generals was abandoned early in 1657 when Cromwell was forced to sack them.

Division of Power in the Republic

- The Lord Protector ruled the people with Parliament and the Council of State. It was an elected position, but for life.
- Parliament had 400 members from England and 30 each from Scotland and Ireland. It met every three years.
- The Council of State helped rule and advise the Lord Protector. It contained military and civilian members.
- The people, men who owned property worth more than £200, could vote. Women could not vote.

> **Key Point**
>
> Men without property were not allowed to vote in the republic.

> **Quick Test**
>
> 1. Describe why England became a republic.
> 2. Explain how the Barebones Parliament was set up.
> 3. Give two reasons why Cromwell abolished the Barebones Parliament.
> 4. What powers did the Instrument of Government give to Cromwell?
> 5. What was the role of the Major-Generals?

The Interregnum 2

You must be able to:

- Describe the restrictions on freedom under Cromwell's rule
- Explain why Cromwell refused the crown in 1657
- Explain why the monarchy was restored.

Restrictions under Cromwell's Rule

- When Cromwell became Lord Protector, he imposed restrictions on certain activities.
- The Puritans believed that if you worked hard, lived a good life and had a good soul you would go to heaven. For them, this meant refraining from many activities they saw as immoral.
- Restrictions were placed on ale-houses and pubs.
- The theatres were all closed down.
- Dancing, bear-baiting and most sports were banned.
- Festivities at Christmas and Easter were outlawed.
- Swearing was banned and punishable by a fine (and those who kept swearing could be sent to prison).
- Cromwell became unpopular and people became frustrated with the strict rules.
- Cromwell and his MPs also raised taxes and were seen as greedy.

> **Key Point**
>
> In the Puritan period, Sunday was a very special day, a day to reflect on religion rather than indulge yourself.

Cromwell is Offered the Crown

- By 1657 it was clear that stability was required because too many changes in the style of government had taken place and were now proving unpopular.
- Many people remembered the stability of having a king in charge. However, they did not want the Stuarts back on the throne.
- In February 1657, Parliament offered the crown to Cromwell.
- He was attracted by the stability of a monarchy, but he had helped to destroy it. He agonised over the decision for six weeks, but he refused.
- Cromwell had been one of the leaders in executing Charles I, and his supporters could not forget how long and hard they had fought for him.
- Cromwell was also concerned that people would question his motives and suggest that he had secretly longed to be king.
- In a ceremony in June 1657, which was very similar to a royal coronation, Cromwell was re-installed as Lord Protector.
- He was now able to remain as Lord Protector for life and could also choose his own successor.

> **Key Point**
>
> As Lord Protector, Cromwell was now able to choose his own successor.

Statue of Oliver Cromwell.

- At the ceremony, Cromwell sat on King Edward's throne, which had been specially moved from Westminster Abbey. Symbols such as a sword of justice and a sceptre were used.
- From 1657 onwards, Cromwell's health began to decline. It was not clear what would happen to England when Cromwell died.
- It was decided that Cromwell's son, Richard, would inherit the title and become Lord Protector.
- Oliver Cromwell died in September 1658. His son Richard took over, but it was clear that he was not good enough for the job.
- Richard lacked the full support of the army and Parliament.
- In 1659 Richard resigned from the job and a senior army officer, General Monck, brought his army to London.
- The Long Parliament was recalled, the original Parliament from 1640, which contained many supporters of the monarchy.
- It was clear that this Parliament wanted to restore the monarchy.

Restoration of the Monarchy

- Having fled to Europe following defeat to Cromwell in 1651, Charles II was asked to return to England to become king in 1660.
- Charles told Parliament that he was prepared to show mercy to those people who had opposed his father Charles I.
- However, he also ordered that Cromwell's body should be dug up and put on trial as a traitor for the execution of Charles I.
- Cromwell's body was put on trial, found guilty and hung from the gallows at Tyburn. His head was removed and displayed in London.
- Thirteen of the people involved in Charles I's execution were also hanged.
- Royal supporters whose land had been confiscated under Cromwell's rule had it restored.
- The House of Lords and Church of England were both restored; Acts of Parliament made other types of church services illegal. They also stopped anyone who was not a member of the Church of England from becoming an MP, teacher or priest.
- Charles II was greeted with huge enthusiasm on his return to the country. Many people had disliked Cromwell's harsh rule.
- Charles II was a popular king and loved the ceremony of the position.
- He was nicknamed the Merry Monarch for his love of parties, wine and horse racing.

Quick Test

1. Describe three examples of activities Cromwell banned.
2. Describe why Cromwell was becoming unpopular by 1657.
3. Why did Cromwell refuse the crown in 1657?
4. Why did Cromwell's son Richard fail in the role of Lord Protector?
5. Why was Charles II a popular monarch?

Timeline

1649 Execution of King Charles: the monarchy is abolished and England becomes a republic.

1653 Cromwell and his army march to Parliament and close it down.

1653 Cromwell is elected as Lord Protector.

1655 Cromwell divides the country into districts and puts army Major-Generals in charge.

1655–57 The rule of the Major-Generals is established to stop opposition towards Cromwell and to protect law and order.

1657 Cromwell is offered the crown, but refuses. He is given extra powers as Lord Protector.

1658 Cromwell dies of ill health.

1658 Cromwell's son Richard becomes Lord Protector.

1659 Richard resigns as Lord Protector due to lack of support.

1660 Charles II returns from Holland and restores the monarchy.

Review Questions

The Norman Conquest

1 What period of history begins with the Norman Conquest?

_____ [1]

2 Under the feudal system, who owned all the land in England?

_____ [1]

3 Who were the villeins?

_____ [1]

4 When did Hereward the Wake lead a rebellion?

_____ [1]

5 In what ways did Harold, King of the Saxons, have difficulty keeping his throne in 1066?

In your answer you should:
- Give your opinion on the most important reason.
- Discuss other reasons.
- Use evidence and your own knowledge to support your answer.

Write your answer on a separate sheet of paper. [10]

6 How did William use castles to control England from 1066?

In your answer you should:
- Give your opinion of the most important use of castles.
- Give other reasons why castles helped William control England.
- Use evidence and your own knowledge to support your answer.

Write your answer on a separate sheet of paper. [10]

Christendom and the Crusades

1 In what year was Thomas A'Becket murdered?

.... [1]

2 Constantinople was the capital of which Christian Empire?

.... [1]

3 In England, what were abbots in charge of?

.... [1]

4 Who won a great victory at the Battle of Hattin in 1187?

.... [1]

5 Why were heaven and hell important to people in the Middle Ages?

In your answer you should:
- Outline what you think people understood by the terms 'heaven' and 'hell'.
- Use your knowledge to show why heaven and hell were important to people in the Middle Ages.

Write your answer on a separate sheet of paper. [10]

6 Imagine you are a Christian living in the Middle Ages. Explain why it is important to go on a Crusade.

In your answer you should:
- Use your own knowledge to describe briefly what took place on a Crusade.
- Explain at least three reasons why people went on Crusades.

Write your answer on a separate sheet of paper. [10]

Review Questions

Magna Carta

1 Which part of France did John lose in 1214?

.... [1]

2 Who in England was unaffected by Magna Carta?

.... [1]

3 Under Magna Carta, whose agreement did the King need in order to raise taxes?

.... [1]

4 When was the first Parliament called and by who?

.... [1]

5 Explain how Magna Carta limited the power of the King.

In your answer you should:
- Write two paragraphs: the first dealing with your opinion of the most important limit on the King's power, and the second dealing with other limits.
- In each case support your answer with examples from Magna Carta.

Write your answer on a separate sheet of paper. [10]

6 Imagine you are living in the reign of King John. Do you regard him as a good or bad king?

In your answer you should:
- Write two paragraphs: the first giving your opinion of why he could be regarded as a good king, and the second explaining why he could be regarded as a bad king.
- Then give your overall judgement of whether he was, on balance, good or bad.
- Support your answer with facts and figures.

Write your answer on a separate sheet of paper. [10]

The Black Death

1 How was the disease brought to England?

.... [1]

2 What did people use to treat the lumps caused by the disease?

.... [1]

3 Why did many villages disappear between 1350 and 1400?

.... [1]

4 What did the Ordinance of Labour of 1349 try to do?

.... [1]

5 Explain how the Black Death affected life in England in the 100 years after 1350.

In your answer you should:
- Describe the effects of the Black Death.
- Give your opinion as to the most important immediate effects of the Black Death, 1348–1350, and then the most important long-term effects (1350–1450).
- Give your opinion of at least two other effects.
- Use facts and figures to support your answer.

Write your answer on a separate sheet of paper. [10]

6 Imagine you lived in England in 1349. Explain how people's lives were changed by the outbreak of the Black Death.

In your answer you should:
- Describe how the Black Death affected where people lived and worked.
- Explain how it affected individual groups such as foreigners and the Church.
- Use facts and figures to support your answer.

Write your answer on a separate sheet of paper. [10]

Practice Questions

The Peasants' Revolt

1. What led villeins to demand wages?

   _____ [1]

2. Which two advisers did the peasants believe gave poor advice to Richard II?

   _____ [1]

3. How long did the Hundred Years War last?

   _____ [1]

4. Which Kentish priest preached that God had made no rich and poor?

   _____ [1]

5. Do you think Richard II was a weak king?

   In your answer you should:
   • Give your opinion of the most important reason.
   • Compare your opinion with at least two other reasons.
   • Use facts and figures to support your answer.

   Write your answer on a separate sheet of paper.   [10]

6. Explain the causes of the Peasants' Revolt. Which do you think was the most important?

   In your answer you should:
   • Give your opinion of the most important cause.
   • Compare your opinion with other causes.
   • Identify the immediate cause as well as other longer term factors.

   Write your answer on a separate sheet of paper.   [10]

Reformation and Counter-Reformation

1 Which Act of Parliament made Henry VIII Supreme Head of the Church in England?

_____ [1]

2 How many monasteries had Henry dissolved by 1540?

_____ [1]

3 Who did Mary I marry?

_____ [1]

4 How many Protestants were burnt at the stake during Mary I's reign?

_____ [1]

5 How and why did Henry VIII decide to break with Rome?

In your answer you should:
* Give your opinion of the most important reason.
* Identify and explain other reasons.
* Support your answers with facts and figures.

Write your answer on a separate sheet of paper. [10]

6 Explain how Henry VIII changed the way people practised religion in England.

In your answer you should:
* Give your opinion of the most important change.
* Identify and explain other changes.
* Support your answer with facts and figures.

Write your answer on a separate sheet of paper. [10]

Practice Questions

The English Civil War

1 What was 'the eleven years of tyranny'?

_____ [1]

2 What month and year did the English Civil War break out?

_____ [1]

3 What was the first major battle of the war?

_____ [1]

4 Where was Charles I executed?

_____ [1]

5 In your opinion, what was the main cause of the English Civil War?

In your answer you should:
- Give your opinion of the most important cause.
- Compare your opinion to at least two other causes.

Write your answer on a separate sheet of paper. [10]

6 Explain why the Battle of Naseby is often viewed as the most significant battle in the English Civil War.

In your answer you should:
- Explain the outcome of this battle.
- Compare it to at least one other battle.

Write your answer on a separate sheet of paper. [10]

The Interregnum

1 Why did England become a republic in 1649?

_____ [1]

2 How did the Barebones Parliament get its name?

_____ [1]

3 What was the punishment for swearing?

_____ [1]

4 What happened to Cromwell's body?

_____ [1]

5 In your opinion, was Cromwell a successful leader of the country?

In your answer you should:
- Give at least three reasons why he was or was not.
- For what reasons may he have been unpopular?

Write your answer on a separate sheet of paper. [10]

6 Describe what life was like for ordinary people under Cromwell's rule.

In your answer you should:
- Describe at least three negative outcomes for ordinary people.
- Use facts to support your answer.

Write your answer on a separate sheet of paper. [10]

British Transatlantic Slave Trade 1

You must be able to:

- Know how Europeans justified the slave trade
- Describe the way slaves were captured, transported and sold
- Understand what life was like on a plantation.

Origins of Slavery

- Slavery has been around for thousands of years, with the Roman Empire relying heavily on slave labour.
- In the mid-15th century the Portuguese explored Africa and captured a small number of Africans to be used as slaves.
- By 1600 the slave trade was thriving, with 80 per cent of captured Africans being sent to the Americas to work on plantations.
- The Americas is what we now know as the USA, South America and the Caribbean.

Slaves captured in Africa.

Justification for Slavery

- A large workforce was needed in the Americas. Many Native Americans had caught diseases from the European settlers and died.
- Europeans often saw black people as physiologically different, saying that they had smaller brains but were stronger.
- Europeans often claimed Africa was uncivilised, despite a rich culture with brilliant architecture and traditions.
- The university in Timbuktu, West Africa, was renowned for medical excellence.

Capture

- Many slaves were prisoners of war who were sold to Europeans.
- Some African Chiefs traded their own people in exchange for European gunpowder, cloth and jewellery.
- Black people were paid to capture other Africans.

The Triangular Trade

- European ships brought textiles, rum and manufactured goods to Africa.
- From Africa, slaves were shipped to the Americas.
- From the Americas, sugar, tobacco and cotton were shipped to Europe.
- These transatlantic slave trade routes were known as the 'Triangular Trade'.

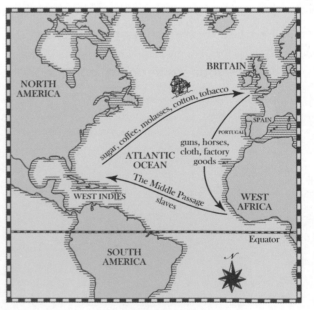

The Triangular Trade.

The Middle Passage

- The journey from Africa to the Americas was known as the 'Middle Passage'.
- This journey was notorious. On large ships it was not uncommon for two-thirds of the slaves to die on the journey.
- Conditions were horrific with hundreds of slaves tightly packed together, often lying in their own waste.
- It was rumoured that slave ships could be smelt when miles away from port.
- Slaves often tried to overthrow the white sailors, but rarely had much success.
- The journey took approximately 12 weeks.
- In 1619, the first group of slaves arrived in Virginia, North America.

> ### Key Point
>
> Between the 15th and 18th centuries at least 12 million African slaves were shipped to the Americas.

Former slaves' living quarters on Shirley Plantation, Virginia.

Slave Auctions

- Slaves were sold at auction when they arrived in the Americas.
- Many families were separated at slave auctions as they were sold to different owners.
- Slaves were often covered in oil or had their cuts filled with tar to make them look healthier and attract a higher price.
- Young women attracted the highest price as they could produce more slaves.
- Young men were the next most popular because of their strength.

Life on the Plantations

- Slave experiences varied depending on their owner, but life on large plantations was generally very difficult.
- They often worked long hours at physically strenuous work such as farming cotton or sugar cane.
- Punishments were brutal, and varied from being whipped or forced to wear a punishment collar, to being sold away from your family, or to being hanged as an example to other slaves.
- Slaves worked hard at keeping their culture alive where they could, such as holding traditional 'jumping the broom' marriage ceremonies or singing African folk songs.

> ### Key Point
>
> There are limited first-hand accounts of the worst plantations because life expectancy was so low.

Sugar cane growing.

> ### Quick Test
>
> 1. In the 15th century where was there a university known for medical excellence?
> 2. What is the estimated minimum number of slaves shipped to the Americas?
> 3. What was this journey known as?
> 4. How were slaves sold?
> 5. Name a slave punishment.

British Transatlantic Slave Trade 2

You must be able to:

- Describe why there was reluctance to end slavery in both Britain and the USA
- Explain how slavery was abolished in Britain
- Explain the role of the Civil War in ending slavery in America.

Opposition to Abolition in Britain

- When the abolitionists first started to campaign to end slavery in the 18th century they faced lots of opposition in Britain.
- This was because many people in Britain directly benefited from slavery.
- In Liverpool many dock workers' jobs were dependent on slavery.
- Factory owners were dependent on both raw materials, such as cotton produced by slaves, and being able to ship their products to the Caribbean.
- The four most prominent anti-campaigners were Thomas Clarkson, Granville Sharp, William Wilberforce and Olaudah Equiano.

Liverpool docks.

Thomas Clarkson

- Thomas Clarkson won a prize for his essay about the horrors of slavery in 1786.
- He devoted over 60 years of his life to campaigning to end slavery.
- With his friend Granville Sharp he founded the Committee for the Abolition of African Slavery.
- He persuaded the MP William Wilberforce to raise the issue in Parliament.

Thomas Clarkson.

Granville Sharp

- In addition to his work with Clarkson, Granville Sharp helped achieve the 1772 ruling that ensured slaves could not be forced back to the colonies once they were in Britain.
- He was motivated after befriending Jonathan Strong, a slave who had been badly treated by his owner, and who was at risk of being sold back into slavery.

William Wilberforce

- William Wilberforce raised the issue of the abolition of slavery 18 times in Parliament, despite much early opposition.

Statue of William Wilberforce.

Olaudah Equiano

- Olaudah Equiano was an ex-slave who bought his freedom.
- He told of the horrors of slavery in his autobiography, published in 1789.

Acts of Abolition

- The Slave Trade Abolition Act of 1807 banned the buying and selling of slaves.
- The Slavery Abolition Act of 1833 abolished slavery completely in the British Empire.

Causes of the American Civil War 1861–65

- For many years the Northern and Southern states of America had been arguing about slavery.
- The Southern economy was dependent on slavery, largely due to the thriving cotton industry.
- Abraham Lincoln was elected President in 1860. He had spoken out against slavery regularly. Tensions heightened and the American Civil War broke out in 1861.
- The Northern states formed the Union Army and the Southern states formed the Confederate Army.

Blacks in the North

- Many black people wanted to fight for the Union Army.
- They were kept separate from white soldiers and paid less.
- Southerners were angry that black soldiers were fighting against them and murdered any they captured.
- Some Northerners began to believe that the war was being fought just for the benefit of black people, which led to lynchings and beatings in some areas.

Blacks in the South

- Many black people fled or helped the Union Army by building shelters and helping the wounded.
- Some defended plantations out of loyalty or fear of their masters.
- The Union Army won the war. The thirteenth amendment abolished slavery in the Americas in 1865.

Quick Test

1. Who was the ex-slave abolitionist in Britain?
2. Who won a prize for his essay against slavery?
3. What did the 1807 Slave Trade Abolition Act achieve?
4. Who became President in 1860?
5. When was slavery abolished in America?

Key Point

The work of the abolitionists changed attitudes. The 1807 Act was passed by 283 votes to 16.

Key Point

The end of slavery did not mean equality. Racist groups such as the Ku Klux Klan emerged soon after the war ended.

Timeline

1441 Portuguese capture a small group of Africans.
1500–1600 Europeans develop colonies in the Americas.
1619 First group of slaves arrive in North America.
1700s Northern states abolish slavery but it remains important in the South.
1807 The Slave Trade Abolition Act in Britain.
1833 The Slavery Abolition Act in Britain.
1861–65 American Civil War.
1865 Slavery is abolished in the Americas.

Britain as the First Industrial Nation 1

You must be able to:

- Understand the factors that caused the Industrial Revolution
- Know what conditions were like for workers in the cities.
- Understand steps taken by some employers to improve life for their workers.

A Period of Rapid Change

- The Industrial Revolution is the title commonly given to the mid-18th century to the late 19th century in Britain.
- This was a time of huge change, with mass migration to the towns and cities. In 1750 approximately 20 per cent of people lived in towns and cities; by 1900 this was 75 per cent.
- Previously the majority of people worked on the land.
- The Industrial Revolution was the result of a combination of factors.
- The population was rising, fuelled in part by improvements in diet and hygiene. The demand for goods was rising with it.
- The traditional method of production, the 'Domestic System', where goods were made in the home, was not meeting demand.
- Coal replaced wood as the leading supply of fuel, and provided three times as much energy.
- It was easy to transport coal as many major mines were near the sea.
- Along with this, massive advancements in science and technology meant that machines were widely produced to be used in factories.
- The development of railways and canals further boosted industry.

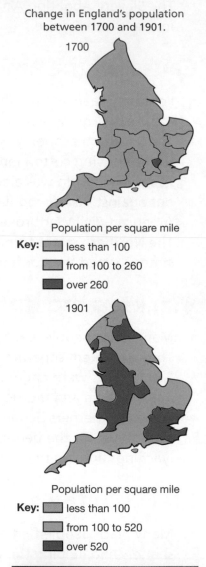

Change in England's population between 1700 and 1901.

1700

Population per square mile

Key:
☐ less than 100
☐ from 100 to 260
■ over 260

1901

Population per square mile

Key:
☐ less than 100
☐ from 100 to 520
■ over 520

Development of Factories

- At first, factories were powered by water wheels.
- This led to Manchester becoming a key industrial city, as fast-running rivers from the Pennines powered industry.
- The textile industry was the first to use this new technology, following Sir Richard Arkwright's invention of the water frame for spinning thread in 1769.
- Eventually the development of the steam engine meant industry was not reliant on water power and so the Industrial Revolution could spread further.

Sir Richard Arkwright.

Life in the Factories

- While machines would eventually mean a reduction in the amount of workers required, for most of the Industrial Revolution the opposite was true.
- Between 1838 and 1885 the number of workers in the cotton industry doubled to 500 000.
- Life for factory workers was often very tough.
- The development of electricity meant that workers were no longer limited to working solely in daylight.
- Many workers worked 14-hour days.
- Machines lacked safety guards, meaning serious injuries were commonplace.
- Scalping was a particularly nasty accident where the top of the scalp was removed as a workers' hair got caught in the mechanisms.
- Children as young as four were used to crawl under machines to collect thread.
- Punishments were brutal and many people, particularly children, were beaten for not working hard enough.

> **Key Point**
>
> The population increase, overcrowding in cities and dangerous conditions in factories reduced life expectancy.

A textile mill in Halifax, West Yorkshire.

Case Study: Josiah Wedgwood

- Not all industrialists treated their workers terribly.
- Some business owners realised if their workers were treated well their productivity would increase.
- Josiah Wedgwood was a potter from Staffordshire.
- While his factories were still strict, he developed a system for his workers similar to modern sick pay.
- He created schools for his workers' children and hospitals to care for the sick.
- He built a village for his workers to live in that was well maintained.
- In return, Wedgwood expected hard work.

> **Key Point**
>
> Wedgwood wasn't the only factory owner to have these ideas. Other notable examples include Arkwright and the Cadbury family.

> **Quick Test**
>
> 1. Who invented the water frame?
> 2. What percentage of people lived in towns and cities by 1900?
> 3. How many workers were there in the cotton industry by 1885?
> 4. How many hours a day did factory workers usually spend working?
> 5. Which potter tried to improve life for his workers?

Britain as the First Industrial Nation 2

You must be able to:

- Understand the effects of the Industrial Revolution on public health
- Understand the importance of the work of Chadwick and Snow
- Describe the intervention put in place by the government to improve public health.

Public Health in the Industrial Era

- Rapid urbanisation brought with it a decline in living standards.
- Manchester's population increased from 18 000 in 1750 to 303 000 in 1851.
- This left many living in inadequate housing.
- Infectious disease was rife. Between 1800 and 1856 one-third of deaths were from tuberculosis.
- There were four major cholera epidemics in London in the 19th century, with the most serious in 1848.
- Around 50 per cent of those who contracted the disease died. It was most common among the working classes.
- People largely believed that disease was caused by 'miasma', meaning bad air. The true cause of disease was not discovered until Louis Pasteur's Germ Theory was published in 1864.
- Several key individuals became concerned and worked tirelessly to improve public health.

> ### Key Point
>
> The theory of miasma had been around since Roman times.

Louis Pasteur.

Edwin Chadwick

- From 1832 Edwin Chadwick was appointed assistant commissioner for the Royal Commission Enquiry on the Poor Laws.
- His first major report, published in 1834, led to the Poor Law Amendment Act in the same year.
- This did not go as far as he wanted it to and he became increasingly concerned by the growth of infectious disease.
- His 1842 report, 'The Sanitary Conditions of the Labouring Population', highlighted the extent of the problems.
- This led to the 1848 Public Health Act, which followed a particularly bad cholera epidemic that frightened the government into action.
- This Act encouraged councils to improve sewers, manage refuse collection, appoint a medical officer for every town and improve access to clean water.
- However, it was only a guideline so wasn't strictly enforced and was abolished 10 years later.
- Many people were worried about how much these public health changes would cost, and many people disliked Chadwick, meaning they were less keen to do what he said.

Underground sewers were improved under the 1848 Public Health Act.

- Chadwick emphasised that improving the health of the working classes would improve the country as a whole, economically and socially.

John Snow

- John Snow was a doctor who became increasingly concerned about the spread of cholera.
- Controversially he refused to accept the idea that miasma caused cholera, and explored the idea that it entered the body through the mouth.
- His ideas were published in his 1849 essay 'On the Mode of Communication of Cholera', following the 1848 epidemic.
- In 1854 he made a breakthrough. He identified a water pump in Broad Street in Soho as the source of an outbreak of cholera.
- He could not prove how cholera was caused until the work of Pasteur in the 1860s. However, the pump handle was removed so people couldn't use the water, and the outbreak diminished.

Public Health Act 1875

- Public health continued to be a key issue for debate. Health remained poor among the working classes, and the Public Health Act of 1875 was introduced to address this.
- Many of the Act's terms were similar to the 1848 Act; however this Act's terms were compulsory.
- Local councils were now made to improve water supplies and sewage systems.
- They were also forced to appoint a Medical Health Officer to monitor conditions.
- Measures were introduced to check that food being sold was safe for consumption.
- Shorter working hours were introduced.
- Fines were created for polluting rivers.
- Steps were taken to clear slum housing and improve living standards.
- While progress was gradual, this Act marked a turning point in government attitudes towards public health, and it recognised the work of people such as Chadwick and Snow.

John Snow identified a hand water pump as a source of cholera.

Key Point

The Public Health Act of 1875 combined and extended a series of smaller Acts.

Timeline

1769 Richard Arkwright invents water frame.
1769 James Watt improves steam engine.
1830 First passenger railway opens.
1848 Public Health Act.
1853 Smallpox vaccination compulsory.
1854 Improvements in hospital hygiene.
1864 Factory Act – to improve standards and safety measures.
1875 Public Health Act.
1894 Manchester ship canal opens.

Quick Test

1. Which disease accounted for one-third of deaths between 1800 and 1856?
2. Which disease did John Snow study in depth?
3. Why was the Public Health Act of 1848 not successful?
4. What could you be fined for under the Public Health Act of 1875?
5. What were shortened under the Public Health Act of 1875?

Democratic Reform 1

You must be able to:

- Explain how the voting system worked in the 1820s
- Explain why the Reform Act was important
- Understand the demands of the Chartists.

The Voting System in the 1820s

- In the 21st century Britain is a democracy where every adult aged 18 or over is allowed to vote. In the 19th century this was not the case.
- Voting was a privilege for only the wealthiest people in society.
- The country was divided into constituencies called counties and boroughs. Most of these sent two MPs to Parliament.
- Before 1832 the right to vote depended on three things:
  - Gender: Only men over the age of 21 were allowed to vote.
  - Property: In order to vote, an individual had to own property over a certain value.
  - Location: The right to vote varied from borough to borough.
- The system was very unfair. In many areas there was no contest because the local landowner was so influential.
- The local landowner could control the election and guarantee that his candidate would win.
- Bribery and threats of violence were common, and voting was not held in secret.
- The poor, the working classes and women were not represented in Parliament.
- Only men could become MPs. They were not paid a salary, so they had to be very rich to become an MP; Parliament was dominated by rich, aristocratic landowners.
- Rotten boroughs were areas that had a small number of voters who could be bribed easily.
- Dunwich in Suffolk was a rotten borough. It had been destroyed and no longer existed, but the 30 people who used to live there still had the right to vote and could elect two MPs.
- Certain areas of Britain, such as the south of England, could elect more MPs than the north. This is because they were far better represented under the voting system.
- Cities such as Manchester, Sheffield and Leeds had no MPs in the 1820s.
- The rapid population growth in the towns and cities meant there was more chance of new political ideas spreading.
- Reformers believed that Parliament no longer represented the country properly and it needed changing.

Voting in 1873.

Industrial city of Sheffield.

The Reform Act 1832

- The first important change to the political system was the 1832 Reform Act.
- This Act achieved two main things:
  - It extended the franchise so that more men could vote.
  - In an attempt to make the system fairer, it got rid of some of the differences in the system that existed across the country.
- The effects of this Act were very limited. Still only a tiny percentage of British men could vote in elections.

The Chartists

- Chartism was a reformist movement that demanded greater change. It had six key demands:
  - A vote for every man aged 21 and over
  - Secret ballots
  - Payment for MPs
  - No property qualifications
  - Annual Parliaments to put an end to bribery and corruption
  - Equal constituencies.
- Chartism was a mass movement with the aim of securing the vote for all men.
- The movement also demanded an improvement in living conditions, increased wages and the end of workhouses. In 1836, a group of London artisans also formed the London Working Men's Association.
- The Charter was signed by over 1.25 million people but when it was presented to Parliament in 1839, MPs ignored it.

The Newport Rising

- In Newport, Wales, approximately 30 000 miners and ironworkers demanded the release of a popular Chartist leader called Henry Vincent.
- Thousands of soldiers were brought in to try and stop the demonstration and eight Chartists were arrested and sentenced to transportation.
- The government believed this showed Chartism was a violent movement and a further 500 Chartists were arrested.

NOT SO *VERY* UNREASONABLE !!! EH?

Cartoon showing the Charter being presented to Lord Russell.

Quick Test

1. Who was allowed to vote in the 1820s?
2. Give one reason why the voting system was unfair.
3. What did the 1832 Reform Act try to achieve?
4. How many people signed the Chartist petition presented in 1839?
5. How many people were arrested during the Newport Rising?

Democratic Reform 2

You must be able to:

- Explain why the Chartist movement failed
- Describe how the 1867 Reform Act increased the vote
- Understand how social reform improved people's lives.

The End of Chartism

- In 1848 the Chartists attempted another petition and said they had collected 6 million signatures. They planned a mass march to Parliament to deliver the petition.
- However only 20 000 people turned up and when the petition was inspected it had 1.9 million signatures rather than 6 million. A number of names had even been forged.
- The meeting and petition were a disaster for the Chartists and it would be another 50 years before the changes they demanded were made.

Prime Minister Benjamin Disraeli.

Social and Political Reforms after 1867

- In 1867 the voting system put in place by the 1832 Reform Act remained intact, but it had come under increasing pressure throughout the 1840s and 1850s from the reformist movements.
- By the early 1860s around 1.5 million men could vote out of a total population of 30 million.
- However, the lack of secret ballots resulted in open voting. This meant that voters could still be offered bribes or intimidated.
- The system was still unfair and did not give equal representation to all areas of Britain.

Parliamentary Reform Act 1867

- This Reform Act increased the number of men able to vote to almost 2.5 million. MPs believed that the working class would not make huge demands on MPs.
- The Prime Minister Benjamin Disraeli claimed that the working class were more interested in 'keeping housed, fed and clothed'.
- The Reform Act did now give most skilled working-class men in the towns the vote, although the vote was still dominated by the middle class.
- The most important change was that people who rented properties could also vote. This resulted in a huge increase in the number of people who could vote – particularly in large towns.

> **Key Point**
>
> The Parliamentary Reform Act increased the number of men who could vote to 2.5 million.

Reforms 1870–71

- In 1870, the government passed the Education Act. This resulted in approximately 3000 to 4000 schools being built for 5–12-year-olds between 1870 and 1880. However, they were not free.
- In 1871, the Bank Holiday Act gave everyone holidays from work by law.
- The Trade Union Act also protected the rights of workers to form a trade union.

Secret Ballot Act 1872

- In 1872 the government introduced the Ballot Act. Voting was now done in secret, in an attempt to deal with the problem of bribery, intimidation and corruption.
- Although this Act failed to end this problem completely, the secret ballot certainly made a difference.
- Polling booths were introduced.

Social Reform 1874–75

- The government passed a number of Acts designed to improve working and living conditions for people.
- The 1874 Factory Act reduced the number of hours people had to work and gave them Saturday afternoon off.
- In 1875 the government passed the Public Health Act. All towns now had to provide clean water and remove sewage and waste.
- The Artisans Dwelling Act encouraged local councils to build better quality housing. The Sale of Food and Medicines Act ensured the quality of food and medicines.

Parliamentary Reform Act 1884

- By the 1880s it was widely recognised that voters in counties deserved the same political rights as those in the boroughs.
- The 1884 Parliamentary Reform Act created a uniform system across the country.
- The right to vote was given to most working men in the countryside as well as towns. About two in three men now had the vote, almost 18 per cent of the total population.

Modern polling booths.

> **Key Point**
>
> The 1884 Parliamentary Reform Act increased the number of men who could vote to 6 million.

> **Timeline**
>
> **1820s** Only men aged over 21 with property can vote.
> **1832** Reform Act.
> **1836** London artisans form the London Working Men's Association.
> **1836** Chartist petition.
> **1839** Newport Uprising.
> **1848** End of Chartism.
> **1867** Reform Act increases the number of men who can vote.
> **1872** Secret Ballot Act attempts to end bribery and corruption.
> **1874** Factory Act reduces working hours.
> **1875** Public Health Act provides clean water in towns.

> **Quick Test**
>
> 1. How many signatures did the Chartists really collect in 1848?
> 2. Why was the 1848 petition a disaster?
> 3. How many men could vote following the Reform Act of 1867?
> 4. How many schools were built between 1870 and 1880?
> 5. How did social reform between 1874 and 1875 improve people's lives?

Women's Suffrage 1

You must be able to:

- Explain how women were treated in the 19th century
- Describe the role of the Suffragette movement
- Understand the role of the Pankhursts in the Suffragette movement.

Women's Rights in the 19th Century

- In Britain during the 19th century women were not allowed to vote and many women believed this was unfair.
- It was assumed that women did not need the vote because their husbands made all the important decisions. A woman's role was seen as taking care of the children and the home.
- Women were often treated as second-class citizens, even if they were married.
- Some examples of rules that women had to live by include:
  - Everything a woman owned passed to her husband when she married.
  - A woman could be forced to stay in a husband's home against her will.
  - A woman could only divorce her husband if she could prove that two of the following had occurred: adultery, cruelty or desertion.
- Women saw the right to vote as an important step towards gaining full equality to men. As a result of the Industrial Revolution and the growth of factories and heavy industry, many women were in full-time employment. This meant they now had opportunities to meet in large organised groups to discuss political and social issues.

Women working in a factory.

Struggle for Equality

- In 1870 and 1882 laws were passed that allowed women to keep their own income and property after they were married.
- This progress had only been made by managing to persuade male members of the Houses of Parliament to pass the laws for them.
- Women were still not allowed to vote or become Members of Parliament.
- 'The Cause' described a movement for women's rights generally. It had no particular political focus.
- In 1872, the National Movement for Women's Suffrage was formed.
- By the end of the 19th century, the issue of gaining the vote had become the focus of women's struggle for equality.

> ### Key Point
>
> In 1903 the women's movement was divided about the best way to protest. Although there were different opinions about methods, they were united in the desire to gain the vote.

The Suffragists – The National Union of Women's Suffrage Societies

- In 1897, various local women's suffrage societies formed the National Union of Women's Suffrage Societies, under the leadership of Millicent Fawcett.
- They wanted the vote for middle-class, property-owning women. They believed the best way to achieve their aims would be to use peaceful tactics such as non-violent demonstrations, petitions and the lobbying of MPs.
- Fawcett believed that if MPs saw the group as intelligent, polite and law-abiding then they would prove that women were responsible enough to gain the vote and participate fully in politics.
- The leadership of the Suffragists was made up of middle-class women but they recognised that in order to have success they needed to gain the support of working-class women also.
- The issue of the vote pulled together women from different sections of society and gave them an identity.
- Millicent Fawcett had to defend her peaceful, non-violent tactics, as a number of women believed that change was taking far too long to arrive.

Millicent Fawcett was the leader of the Suffragist movement.

Suffragettes fought for women to be given the vote.

The Suffragettes – Women's Social and Political Union

- The Women's Social and Political Union was founded by Emmeline Pankhurst and her daughters Christabel and Sylvia in 1903. The Suffragettes were born out of the Suffragist movement.
- Emmeline Pankhurst had been a member of the Manchester Suffragist group but had become angered by the lack of action and slow pace of change.
- The Pankhursts felt that women had waited too long to be given the vote and decided that direct action would be more effective. They believed it was a women's right to be given the vote.
- They believed it would take an active organisation, with young working-class women, to draw attention to their demands.
- The motto of the Suffragettes was '*Deeds not words*' and from 1912 onwards their campaigning became more violent.
- Law-breaking, violence and hunger strikes were all considered acceptable campaign tactics.

> ## Key Point
>
> The Pankhursts believed that direct action was the way to gain popularity for their cause.

Emmeline Pankhurst's portrait on a British stamp.

Quick Test

1. For what reasons could women get divorced in the 19th century?
2. What law was passed in 1870?
3. Who was the leader of the Suffragists?
4. Who founded the Women's Social and Political Union?
5. What was the motto of the Suffragettes?

Women's Suffrage 2

You must be able to:

- Explain the methods used by the Suffragette movement
- Describe how the Cat and Mouse Act gained sympathy for the Suffragette movement
- Understand how women finally gained the vote.

Actions of the Suffragette Movement

- In 1905 two members of the Suffragettes, Christabel Pankhurst and Annie Kenney, interrupted a meeting in Manchester to ask two politicians, Winston Churchill and Sir Edward Grey, if they believed women should have the right to vote.
- The two women then got out a banner that said 'Votes for Women' and shouted at the two politicians to answer their questions.
- Pankhurst and Kenney were thrown out of the meeting and arrested for causing an obstruction and assaulting a police officer.
- In 1906, 30 women went to Downing Street and asked to see the Prime Minister.
- After banging on the door and demanding to be let in, two of the women tried to rush inside, but were arrested.
- A third woman was arrested after jumping on the Prime Minister's car and attempting to address the crowd.
- In 1908 a protest rally was held in Hyde Park. Estimates suggest that between 250 000 and 500 000 people attended.
- In 1909 Marion Wallace Dunlop was sentenced to prison for defacing a wall of St. Stephen's Church. She asked to be treated as a political prisoner.
- This request was denied so she began a hunger strike lasting 91 hours. She was then released from prison.

Poster in support of votes for women.

Cat and Mouse Act

- When a Suffragette was sent to prison, it was assumed that she would go on hunger strike as this gained maximum publicity.
- The Cat and Mouse Act allowed the Suffragettes to go on a hunger strike and let them get weaker and weaker.
- When the Suffragettes were very weak they were then released from prison.
- Those who were released were so weak that they could take no part in any violence. When they had regained their strength, they were re-arrested and the whole process started again.
- Hunger strikers were force fed by prison doctors using steel mouth clamps and tubes. This was a painful and brutal process.
- Force feeding shocked the public and gained a lot of sympathy for the Suffragettes and their cause.

Key Point

The government's use of the Cat and Mouse Act shocked many people because of its brutality towards women.

Increasing Violence

- In 1911, 220 women were arrested after a series of violent acts that included breaking windows at government offices.
- There were also acts of violence targeted at the Home Office, Treasury and *Daily Mail* newspaper.
- In 1912, Mary Leigh threw a small axe into the Prime Minister's carriage.
- Mary Leigh also tried to burn down the Theatre Royal.
- The curtains were set alight, a flaming chair was thrown into the orchestra and a number of small bombs made out of tin cans were set off.
- Leigh was arrested and sentenced to five years in prison.
- In June 1913, Emily Wilding Davison attended the Epsom Derby horse race. As the King's horse was racing past, Emily ran onto the race track and was knocked down by the horse.
- She suffered a fractured skull and died without regaining consciousness.
- Her funeral was a huge public spectacle and generated lots of publicity for the Suffragette movement.

Gaining the Vote

- When the First World War broke out many women took on the jobs that had been left by men going off to fight. They proved they could do these jobs just as well as men.
- The Suffragettes used this to publicise the important role that women were playing, even though they disagreed with the war.
- They began to reduce their more violent activities due to the war and its effect on the nation.
- The Suffragists supported the war but saw it as an opportunity to put pressure on the government.
- The government had to introduce a new voting law to allow soldiers and sailors fighting in the war to be able to vote.
- The Suffragists argued that women should also be included in the new law as they had done so much to help the war effort.
- In 1918, women over the age of 30 who owned property were given the right to vote, and by 1928 this was extended to include all women.

Quick Test

1. What happened to Christabel Pankhurst and Annie Kenney in 1905?
2. How many people attended the protest rally in Hyde Park?
3. What did Mary Leigh try to do in 1912?
4. How did Emily Wilding Davison die in 1913?
5. In what year were all women given the vote?

Key Point

The Suffragette movement suspended many of its more violent actions during the war. It was fearful of a backlash from the public during wartime.

Timeline

1870 Law passed to allow women to keep income and property after marriage.
1872 National Movement for Women's Suffrage formed.
1897 Millicent Fawcett forms the National Union of Women's Suffrage Societies.
1903 Women's Social and Political Union formed by the Pankhursts.
1905 Two members of the Suffragette movement arrested in Manchester.
1906 Protest at Downing Street.
1908 Protest rally in Hyde Park.
1911 220 women arrested for a series of violent protests.
1913 Emily Davison killed by a horse at the Epsom Derby.
1918 Women over 30 who own property given the right to vote.
1928 All women given the right to vote in Britain.

Review Questions

The Peasants' Revolt

1 How many peasants were involved in the revolt?

.... [1]

2 What did the rebels do on entering London?

.... [1]

3 Who did the rebels murder?

.... [1]

4 How many rebels were killed?

.... [1]

5 Explain why the Peasants' Revolt failed.

In your answer you should:
- Give your own opinion of the most important reason.
- Identify and explain at least two other reasons.
- Support your answer with facts and figures.

Write your answer on a separate sheet of paper. [10]

6 Explain how you think the Peasants' Revolt changed life in England in the 100 years after 1381.

In your answer you should:
- Give your opinion of the most important change.
- Identify at least two other changes.
- Support your answer with facts and figures.

Write your answer on a separate sheet of paper. [10]

Reformation and Counter-Reformation

1 How old was Edward VI when he became King?

_____ [1]

2 What did Edward VI remove from churches?

_____ [1]

3 What was the Pilgrimage of Grace?

_____ [1]

4 Which appointments did Henry take over from the Pope?

_____ [1]

5 Why do you think Henry VIII dissolved (closed) the monasteries?

In your answer you should:
- Give your opinion of the most important reason.
- Support your opinion with facts and figures.
- Compare your choice with other reasons.

Write your answer on a separate sheet of paper. [10]

6 In what ways did religious changes under Edward VI differ from those under Henry VIII?

In your answer you should:
- Give your own opinion of the major difference.
- Identify and explain other differences.
- Support your answer with facts and figures.

Write your answer on a separate sheet of paper. [10]

Review Questions

The English Civil War

Write your answers to the following questions on a separate sheet of paper.

1 What was Charles I's wife called? [1]

2 Name an unpopular adviser to Charles I. [1]

3 How many men did each side lose at Edgehill? [1]

4 What was the name of the chief judge at Charles's trial? [1]

5 Study the source below. It shows a painting of Charles's execution from 1649.

What useful information does it give you? What are its drawbacks? [5]

6 In your opinion, how important was the role of Oliver Cromwell in the English Civil War?

In your answer you should:
- Assess the importance of his military skill and the development of the New Model Army.
- Evaluate his role in the trial and execution of Charles I. [10]

The Interregnum

Write your answers to the following questions on a separate sheet of paper.

1 What event occurred on 30 January 1649? [1]

2 What was the function of the Council of State? [1]

3 How often was Parliament to meet, and stay in session for? [1]

4 Who recalled the Long Parliament following Cromwell's death? [1]

5 Describe how the country was governed between 1649 and 1653.

In your answer you should:
- Describe at least three ways that power was divided between different groups.
- Use facts to support your answer. [10]

6 Study the source below, which shows Cromwell and Parliament.

How useful is this for understanding Cromwell's rule during the Interregnum? What are its drawbacks? Give reasons for your answer. [5]

British Transatlantic Slave Trade

1 Where did 80 per cent of captured Africans get sent to work?

.... [1]

2 What type of slaves usually sold for the most money?

.... [1]

3 When did Britain abolish the slave trade?

.... [1]

4 Between what years did the American Civil War take place?

.... [1]

5 Describe what life was like for a slave from capture to arriving on a plantation.

In your answer you should:
- Give information about how they might have become a slave.
- Details about the Middle Passage and slave auctions.

Write your answer on a separate sheet of paper. [10]

Slaves at work on a plantation.

6 Who was the most important abolitionist? Explain your answer.

In your answer you should:
- Explain the roles of the abolitionists.
- Give a judgement about the most important.

Write your answer on a separate sheet of paper. [10]

Britain as the First Industrial Nation

1 What became the leading fuel in the industrial era?

.... [1]

2 Who made an improved steam engine?

.... [1]

3 There were four epidemics of which disease in 19th-century London?

.... [1]

4 Which Act was introduced in 1848 and improved upon in 1875?

.... [1]

5 Describe the reasons for the start of the Industrial Revolution.

In your answer you should:
Give details of at least three factors contributing to industrialisation in Britain.

Write your answer on a separate sheet of paper. [10]

6 Explain the dangers faced by workers in the cities.

In your answer you should:
* Look at the risks in factories.
* Consider the risks from living conditions.

Write your answer on a separate sheet of paper. [10]

Practice Questions

Democratic Reform

1 In what year did the Reform Act take place?

.... [1]

2 What was a rotten borough?

.... [1]

3 How many people were allowed to vote in the early 1860s?

.... [1]

4 What Act did the government pass in 1872?

.... [1]

5 In your opinion, why did the voting system need reforming by 1832?

In your answer you should:
- Give at least three examples of unfairness in the voting system.
- Use facts to support your answer.

Write your answer on a separate sheet of paper. [10]

6 Explain whether the Chartist movement should be viewed as a failure.

In your answer you should:
- Explain at least three different negative outcomes for the Chartist movement.
- Use facts to support your answer.

Write your answer on a separate sheet of paper. [10]

Women's Suffrage

1 Why were women not allowed to vote?

.... [1]

2 What law was passed in 1870?

.... [1]

3 What year did Marion Wallace Dunlop begin her hunger strike in prison?

.... [1]

4 Which type of women were given the vote in 1918?

.... [1]

5 In your opinion, how important was the role of the Pankhursts in the suffrage campaign?

In your answer you should:
- Describe the actions of the Suffragette Movement.
- Take into account other factors involved in the suffrage campaign.
- Use facts to support your answer.

Write your answer on a separate sheet of paper. [10]

6 Explain why the struggle for equality failed in the 19th century.

In your answer you should:
- Give your opinion on at least three different reasons.
- Use facts to support your answer.

Write your answer on a separate sheet of paper. [10]

The First World War 1

You must be able to:

- Explain the causes of the war
- Describe the alliances and opposing forces
- Understand the nature of trench warfare
- Explain why the Gallipoli campaign was a disaster for Britain.

The Assassination of Archduke Franz Ferdinand

- Archduke Franz Ferdinand was next in line to the Austrian throne.
- He was killed in June 1914 by a Serbian extremist, Gavrilo Princip, who was a member of the Black Hand terrorist gang.
- Serbians were annoyed by the treatment of Serbs living in Bosnia, which had been Serbian but was part of Austria-Hungary at this time.
- The assassination led to Austria-Hungary declaring war on Serbia, which triggered a response from Europe's alliance system.

Site of Franz Ferdinand's assassination, Sarajevo, Bosnia.

Alliances

- Russia had an agreement to support Serbia should it go to war.
- Germany had an agreement to support Austria-Hungary should it go to war.
- Britain and France had an agreement to support Russia should it go to war.
- This meant many countries were drawn into the war.

Arms Race

- There was a long history of rivalry between Britain and Germany.
- Britain had built a new, powerful warship called the Dreadnought.
- Germany responded by building their own Dreadnoughts.
- This triggered a competition to have the most powerful navy, known as the arms race.
- This was important as it made both countries paranoid that the other was preparing for war.

A Dreadnought warship.

Empires

- Britain had a big empire that Germany was jealous of, causing tension.
- Many European countries were competing to make their empires bigger.

> **Key Point**
>
> War broke out in August 1914. By November 1918, 20 million soldiers were dead.

Trench Warfare

- Trench warfare was a recent development.
- Hundreds of miles of trenches were dug across Europe, with the aim of protecting soldiers from enemy shelling.
- Conditions in the trenches were often very bad, and a condition called trench foot developed in which soldiers' feet began to rot due to the mud and bacteria.
- Generals struggled to keep up with advances in technology such as machine guns, tanks and poison gas, and many were heavily criticised for their tactics.

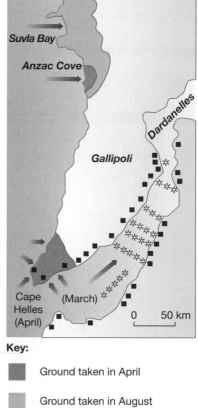

Soldiers in a trench.

Cross-section of a First World War trench.

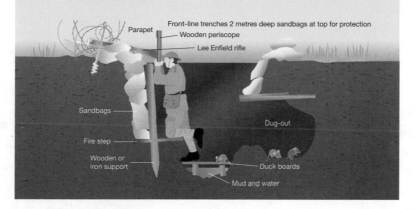

The Gallipoli campaign.

The Gallipoli Campaign

- The Western Front was in stalemate in February 1915.
- Soldiers from Britain and the Empire went to help the Russians who were being threatened by the Turks at Caucasus.
- The British planned a naval campaign centred around the Gallipoli peninsula in the Dardanelles to divert troops from Caucasus.
- Bad weather meant six British ships were destroyed or damaged before arrival.
- The Turks knew the British were on their way and so massively increased their numbers before they arrived.
- The aim was to get Turkey out of the war and to get some of the Balkan states to join the Allies.
- The campaign was a failure. Heat and disease made conditions difficult for the British soldiers.
- In December 1915 the campaign was abandoned. Troops started to go home as little progress was made. In total, 300 000 Turkish and 214 000 Allied soldiers died.

Key:

- Ground taken in April
- Ground taken in August
- ■ Turkish fort
- ✳ Turkish mines
- ➡ Allied attacks

Quick Test

1. Whose assassination triggered the start of the war?
2. Why were some Serbians angry with Austria-Hungary?
3. What was the name of the new warship?
4. What were the new types of technology used in the war?
5. What factors contributed to Britain failing at Gallipoli?

Key Point

The disaster of Gallipoli contributed to Lloyd George replacing Asquith as Prime Minister in 1916.

The First World War 2

You must be able to:

- Describe where the key battles took place
- Explain why the tactics of the war were controversial
- Understand the consequences of the war.

Battle of Verdun (February–July 1916)

- In February 1916, German General von Falkenhayn decided the key to winning the war was Western France.
- He knew the French would use many soldiers to protect the historically important fortress town of Verdun.
- Falkenhayn believed he could damage the French army.
- However, the French were well led and well prepared.
- Throughout March and April land near Verdun changed hands many times, with the French led by General Pétain.
- The battle ended in July 1916 as the Allies began the Somme offensive, partly to relieve the French.
- Approximately 400 000 soldiers from each side were killed.
- By October, Verdun and the surrounding area was completely back in French hands.

Battle of the Somme (July–November 1916)

- The Battle of the Somme began in July 1916.
- The first day was the worst ever in British military history with 20 000 dead and 20 000 injured.
- British General Haig refused to change tactics.
- Men were instructed to walk slowly over 'No Man's Land' resulting in many being killed by German machine guns.
- They were trying to take over a 15-mile stretch of trenches, but by November had advanced only 5 miles.
- Groups of friends fighting in 'Pals Battalions' were wiped out, meaning some communities lost most of their young men.
- In all, 420 000 British soldiers died along with 195 000 French and 650 000 Germans.
- Although the British lost fewer men than the Germans, the battle is often seen as disastrous in British military history.

Verdun memorial cemetery.

Key Point

No Man's Land was the land between trenches not owned by either side.

Key:

- ⌇ German front line
- ⌇ British / French front line
- ⌇ Support trench
- ⌇ Reserve trench
- ⌇ 'Saps' – observation posts, machine gun positions, etc
- ⌇ Barbed wire
- ⌇ Communication trenches

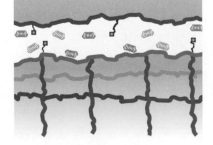

No Man's Land.

End of the War

- The war ended on 11 November 1918 when Germany surrendered.
- In all, 8 million soldiers and 9 million civilians had died.

Treaty of Versailles

- A treaty was made on 28 June 1919 to punish Germany for losing the war.
- It was signed at the Palace of Versailles, just outside Paris, after six months of negotiations.
- Germany was banned from the talks.
- The Treaty angered the German people and was later used as propaganda by extremists in Germany.

Terms of the Treaty

Military Restrictions

- German army to be reduced to 100 000 men.
- No soldiers in Rhineland.
- No air force.
- No submarines.
- Just six battleships.

Reparations

- Germany to pay £6.6 billion to the Allies for damage caused by the war.

War Guilt Clause (Article 231)

- Germany had to take all the blame for starting the war.

Territorial Losses

- Germany to give Alsace-Lorraine back to France.
- To lose its entire empire.
- To give back Upper Silesia to Poland, separating Prussia from the rest of Germany (known as the Polish Corridor).
- To lose important industrial areas such as the Saar where there were many coalfields.

Quick Test

1. Who was seen as a hero after Verdun?
2. Who led the British at the Somme?
3. Why did some communities back in Britain lose all their young men?
4. How much money did Germany have to pay to the Allies?
5. What is Article 231 often known as?

Key Point

Propaganda is information and ideas (true or false) deliberately spread to support a particular group or political view.

Inside the Palace of Versailles.

Timeline

June 1914 Franz Ferdinand assassinated.
August 1914 War breaks out.
Feb–Dec 1915 Gallipoli campaign.
1916 Lloyd George becomes Prime Minister.
Feb–July 1916 The Battle of Verdun.
July–Nov 1916 The Battle of the Somme.
11 November 1918 The war ends.
28 June 1919 The Treaty of Versailles signed.

The Second World War 1

You must be able to:

- Explain the causes of the war
- Describe Hitler's aims between 1933 and 1939
- Understand how the treatment of Jews changed between 1933 and 1945.

Hitler's Aims

- Adolf Hitler became Chancellor of Germany in 1933. He was later elected as dictator (Führer) of Nazi Germany.
- Hitler's aims between 1933 and 1939 were:
  - the reunion of Germany and Austria
  - the cancellation of the Treaty of Versailles
  - rearmament and the return of land taken away by the Treaty of Versailles
  - to destroy Communism
  - to gain land in the East, Russia and Eastern Europe for the German people – *Lebensraum* (living space).

Rearmament

- From 1933, Hitler began to secretly build up his army and air force. This had been banned by the Treaty of Versailles.
- Britain and France did nothing to prevent this from happening. They were more worried about the power of the Soviet Union.

The Rhineland and Austria

- In 1936, Hitler ordered his troops to march into the Rhineland, which was forbidden by the Treaty of Versailles.
- Many people thought it was reasonable for Germany to have troops protecting its own land.
- In 1938 Hitler sent troops into Austria and forced the Austrian leader to hold a vote on unification.
- Britain, France and Italy had refused to help Austria because they did not want to risk the possibility of war.
- Hitler promised that he wanted peace in Europe.

The Sudetenland and Czechoslovakia

- In September 1938 Hitler demanded that the Sudetenland area of Czechoslovakia unite with Germany.
- Hitler claimed that people who lived there were German and wanted to unite with Germany.

Adolf Hitler.

> **Key Point**
>
> Although the Treaty of Versailles had forbidden Germany to rearm, Hitler ignored this. From 1933 onwards he began to rearm Germany in preparation for war.

- The British Prime Minister, Neville Chamberlain, visited Hitler three times to attempt to prevent war.
- This policy was known as appeasement. They signed the Munich Pact. Chamberlain declared that this was 'peace in our time'.
- Chamberlain agreed that Hitler could keep the Sudetenland if he promised not to take over the rest of Czechoslovakia.
- In March 1939 Hitler broke the Munich Pact and German troops invaded the rest of Czechoslovakia.

Poland

- In August 1939, Germany and the Soviet Union signed a non-aggression agreement called the Nazi–Soviet Pact.
- On 1 September 1939 Hitler invaded Poland.
- Britain and France declared war on Germany on 3 September 1939.

German aggression up to September 1939.

The Holocaust

- After 1933, the persecution of Jewish people became commonplace.
- On 9th November 1938, there was a night of violent attacks on Jews and their homes, businesses and synagogues. This is known as *Kristallnacht* (night of broken glass).
- Once the war had begun, the persecution increased. Jews in Germany and occupied countries were rounded up and sent to ghettos. Around 500,000 Polish Jews died of disease and starvation in the ghettos.
- A policy called the 'Final Solution' saw Jews moved into concentration camps, where many died or were executed in gas chambers. The most infamous camps included Auschwitz and Treblinka.
- By the end of the war over six million Jewish people had been killed, along with thousands of other victims of persecution. This is known as the Holocaust.

> ### Key Point
> The policy of appeasement failed because Hitler failed to keep his word and invaded Czechoslovakia and Poland.

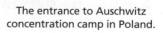

The entrance to Auschwitz concentration camp in Poland.

> ### Quick Test
> 1. Why did Britain and France fail to prevent Hitler from rearming?
> 2. How did Hitler manage to unite Germany and Austria?
> 3. Why did Hitler demand back the Sudetenland?
> 4. Why did the policy of appeasement fail?
> 5. What was the 'Final Solution'?

The Second World War 2

You must be able to:

- Explain why the Battle of Britain was a success
- Describe why Hitler wanted to invade the Soviet Union
- Understand how the war came to an end.

War in Europe

- On 1 September 1939 Germany invaded Poland.
- On 3 September Britain declared war on Germany.
- By April 1940 Germany had invaded Holland and France. The speed of the German attacks – known as *Blitzkrieg* (lightning war) – took the Allies by surprise.
- British and French troops had been pushed back to the beaches of Dunkirk. They were now trapped between the German army and the English Channel. The only chance of escape was by sea.
- In May 1940 the British government put a plan into action known as Operation Dynamo.
- The aim was to evacuate 300 000 soldiers by ship from the beaches of Dunkirk.
- The Royal Navy was used to transport men safely from Dunkirk, and many soldiers were rescued using fishing boats and pleasure steamers.
- Dunkirk is seen as a great success and a plan of courage and resilience. But it also highlighted the power, force and speed of the German army.

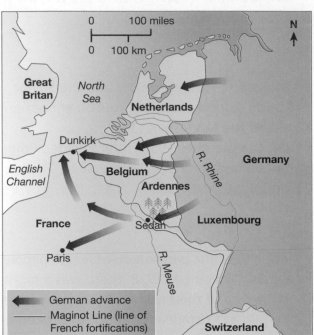

German invasion of France.

Battle of Britain

- After Dunkirk Hitler controlled all of Western Europe. He then made preparations to invade Britain – Operation Sealion.
- The first task was to use the German air force – the Luftwaffe – to wipe out the British air force – the RAF.
- If Hitler managed this he could then send soldiers across the Channel in ships.
- The Germans believed the Luftwaffe was superior to the RAF.
- In reality, the air forces were evenly matched and Britain had developed a radar system to detect German planes before they reached the English coast.
- Although the Germans bombed many airfields, ports and radar stations they could not defeat the RAF.
- Hitler called off Operation Sealion after two months. The invasion of Britain had been prevented, and Hitler had suffered his first defeat of the war.

Key Point

The early war in Europe demonstrated the strength of the German army. However, the Battle of Britain marked an important turning point as Britain resisted the German attack.

War in the East

- Hitler wanted to invade the Soviet Union to defeat Communism and take over land in Russia to use for German people. Hitler believed the Soviets could be defeated in six weeks.
- An army of 3 million men was able to rapidly surround the Soviet army and capture the most important Russian cities of Moscow and Leningrad.
- However, the Soviets fought fiercely and prevented the Germans advancing any further.
- The harsh Russian winter proved to be a disaster for the Germans. Many German soldiers froze to death as the temperature dropped to minus 40 degrees.

Battle of Stalingrad

- After the winter, Hitler ordered his troops to capture Stalingrad.
- This was a brutal battle, but the Soviet army gradually began to take control of Stalingrad and surrounded the German army.
- The Germans were now cut off from their supply chain and forced to surrender.
- This is seen as a turning point in the war as the Soviet army now began to advance towards Germany.

End of the War

- The Germans were fighting on both the Western and Eastern fronts and were rapidly running out of soldiers and supplies.
- On 6 June 1944 the D-Day invasion took place. Nearly 200 000 British and American soldiers landed in Normandy, northern France, and began advancing through France towards Germany.
- The German army was being pushed further back towards Germany as the British and Americans took control of Western Europe and the Soviets took control of Eastern Europe.
- By 1945 it was clear to Hitler and his army that they were going to be defeated.
- By April the British, Americans and Soviets were within days of reaching Berlin and forcing Hitler to surrender.
- On 30 April 1945 Hitler committed suicide. The war was over. Germany surrendered.

Quick Test

1. What is Blitzkrieg?
2. How did the British army escape from Dunkirk?
3. What is the name of the German air force?
4. How many soldiers did Hitler send to fight Russia?
5. How many soldiers landed at Normandy on D-Day?

Key Point

Despite the harsh conditions and extreme brutality of the Battle of Stalingrad, this proved to be a major turning point in the war, as Germany suffered defeat to the Soviet Union.

Timeline

1933 Germany begins to rearm.
1936 German troops march into the Rhineland.
1938 Austria and Germany unite.
1938 Appeasement agreement (Munich Pact).
1939 Hitler invades Czechoslovakia and Poland.
1939 Britain and France declare war on Germany.
1940 Evacuation of Dunkirk.
1940 Battle of Britain.
1941 Germany invades the Soviet Union.
1942 Russia starts to push the German army backwards.
1943 German army surrenders at Stalingrad.
1944 D-Day landings.
1945 Germany surrenders and the war is over.

The Creation of the Welfare State 1

You must be able to:

- Understand the economic, political and social reasons behind the reforms
- Describe the main Liberal reforms
- Explain the successes of these reforms
- Explain the limitations of these reforms.

Background – Need for Reform

- Prior to the 20th century the government had a 'laissez-faire' approach to welfare. This meant that it didn't believe it was the role of the state to intervene in people's lives.
- The work of social investigators, such as Edwin Chadwick, Charles Booth and Joseph Rowntree, increasingly drew attention to the need for state support for the poor.
- Chadwick had been working in London in the mid-19th century and drew attention to many public health issues, particularly the link between dirty water and cholera.
- Booth was working in London at the end of the 19th century, and discovered 35 per cent of the population there lived below the poverty line.
- The poverty line, or bread line, is the amount of money people need to buy essentials such as food, shelter and basic clothing.
- Seebohm Rowntree built upon the work of his father Joseph. In 1901, he wrote a report showing that 28 per cent of people were living below the poverty line in York.
- In 1899, two-thirds of those signing up to fight in the Boer War were unfit for service.
- Germany had overtaken Britain as an industrial power; it had a strong welfare system for workers.
- The Labour Party was emerging and advertising itself as the 'voice of the working class'. Its manifesto focused heavily on welfare reform.
- The power of trade unions was strengthening, and they demanded better conditions for workers.
- This was a genuine threat to the Liberal government.
- David Lloyd George, Chancellor of the Exchequer from 1906, genuinely wanted to improve the lives of the poor.
- In 1910, however, the Liberal Party did not get a majority and had to form a coalition (a joint government) with Labour.
- Between 1910 and 1912 a series of strikes threatened to bring British industry to a halt, for example the Coal Strike of 1912.

Key Point

The government was not just motivated by sympathy for the poor. It realised there was a large threat to Britain's economic status and national security if the condition of the workers and the army did not improve.

David Lloyd George.

Coal mine.

Introduction of Reforms

- Seebohm Rowntree highlighted the three times when people were most vulnerable in their lifetime: childhood, old age, and times of unemployment or sickness.
- The majority of reforms were intended to address these issues.

Children's Reforms	Successes	Limitations
1906 Free School Meals Act.	Ensured one good meal a day.	Wasn't compulsory, many councils didn't provide them.
1907 School Medical Inspectors Act.	Monitored the health of all school children.	Limited access to health care if there was a problem.

Reforms for the Elderly	Successes	Limitations
1908 Old Age Pensions Act.	5s a week for the over 70s or 7s a week for married couples. Fewer people went to the workhouse.	Life expectancy was around 45 for most workers – few people lived to be 70. It was not enough money to live on. You couldn't claim if you had never worked.

Reforms for Workers	Successes	Limitations
1909 Labour Exchanges set up.	By 1914 had helped 1 million find work.	Often part-time, temporary or badly paid jobs.
1911 National Insurance Act.	Free health care for workers. Paid workers if they were sick or unemployed.	Health care did not extend to the worker's family. The 7s 6d a week it paid out was not enough to support a family. Only paid for a limited time.

> ## Revise
>
> ### Key Point
>
> There were many more reforms at the time; the tables show those often seen as most important. However, many people felt the reforms did not go far enough.

Children receiving free school meals today.

Workers receiving free health care.

Quick Test

1. Who was Chancellor of the Exchequer from 1906?
2. Who wrote a report showing poverty in York?
3. How old did you have to be to claim a pension?
4. When were free school meals introduced?
5. How many people had found work with the Labour Exchanges by 1914?

The Creation of the Welfare State 2

You must be able to:

- Understand the impact of the Second World War on welfare reform
- Understand the importance of the Beveridge Report
- Explain the significance of the creation of the NHS
- Know about other welfare reforms that were a result of the Beveridge Report.

Impact of the Second World War

- The Second World War highlighted the need for further welfare measures.
- People had become more accepting of state involvement in their lives. This had been necessary for the war effort with measures such as rationing.
- The evacuation programme had made people aware of the appalling poverty some children were growing up in.
- Health care had become more organised.
- One thousand operating theatres had been opened to cope with the effects of the air raids.
- In addition to this, many temporary hospitals had opened, along with blood transfusion and ambulance services.
- In 1942, the Beveridge Report was published, highlighting the problems Britain faced and outlining solutions.

Ration books.

Beveridge Report

- William Beveridge was an economist (financial expert) and social reformer.
- He developed a theory of the 'Five Giants of Evil' that Britain needed to overcome if it was to recover from the war.
- He also offered solutions of how this could be achieved.

Key Point

Beveridge published his report in 1942, but his recommendations were not acted upon immediately.

Giant	Problems it was Causing	Solution
Want	Poverty.	Improving National Insurance.
Disease	Unhealthy workforce.	Free health care for all.
Squalor	Unfit living conditions, slum housing.	Social housing.
Ignorance	Inequality in education.	Raising the school leaving age to 15; better school meals.
Idleness	Unemployment.	Work creation schemes to rebuild Britain.

Creation of the NHS

- Aneurin Bevan, Health Minister in the post-war Labour government, set up the National Health Service (NHS) in 1948.
- He intended it to be:
  - Universal: everyone could use it regardless of their circumstances.
  - Comprehensive: to cover all services including dentists and opticians.
  - Free at the point of need: patients would not pay; National Insurance contributions would fund it.
- An ambulance service was to be set up to cover emergencies.

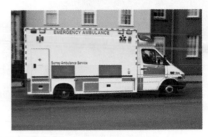

An ambulance today

Opposition to the NHS

- Before he could create the NHS, Bevan had to overcome opposition from doctors.
- Many doctors were worried about losing money, so he agreed to them treating private as well as NHS patients.
- He is said to have 'stuffed their throats with gold' by giving them a high salary.

Problems with the NHS

- It was very expensive; National Insurance didn't cover the costs so it also had to be funded from taxes.
- Certain services soon had to be paid for; for example prescription charges were introduced in 1951.

Successes of the NHS

- Life expectancy has improved considerably since the NHS was established.
- Many childhood diseases, such as polio, have been eradicated as a result of vaccination programmes.
- It is seen as the 'jewel in the crown' of social reform.

Key Point

The NHS wasn't the only result of the Beveridge Report. Other important Acts are shown on the timeline.

Timeline

1906 Free school meals.
1907 School Medical Inspectors Act.
1908 Children's Charter and old age pensions.
1909 Labour Exchanges set up.
1911 National Insurance Act.
1944 Education Act (implemented 1945); school leaving age raised to 15.
1945 Family allowances introduced.
1946 National Insurance Act extended.
1948 NHS introduced.
1948 National Assistance Act to help those not covered by National Insurance.

Quick Test

1. Who spoke about the 'Five Giants of Evil' in his report?
2. Name the 'Five Giants of Evil'.
3. Who was Health Minister when the NHS was created?
4. What was the school leaving age raised to in 1944?
5. What was introduced in 1951?

Britain's Place in the World 1945–Present 1

You must be able to:

- Describe reasons why the population changed after 1945
- Explain the decline of traditional industries in the post-war period
- Understand the cultural changes since 1945.

Post-war Changes

- Immediately after the Second World War, Britain saw enormous social change. The country was bankrupt after the war.
- The wartime Prime Minister Winston Churchill was voted out. The new Labour government nationalised many industries including electricity, gas, water and health.
- Britain took a long time to recover and food rationing continued until 1954.
- In the 1950s, rebuilding continued. A steady flow of immigrants from Commonwealth nations began, mainly from the Caribbean and the Indian subcontinent.
- In 1956 Britain and France lost control of the Suez Canal during the Suez Crisis. It was clear that Britain was no longer a superpower.
- India and Pakistan gained their independence in 1947.
- Britain knew it could no longer afford its large empire. By 1970 it had withdrawn from almost all its colonies.

The Suez Canal in Egypt.

Population Changes

- Between 1948 and 1997 the population of Britain rose from 47 million to 58 million. The biggest reason for this population increase was more advanced medical care.
- The NHS had been set up in 1948 to provide free health care for everyone.
- Following the Second World War, Britain needed more workers to help rebuild the nation. A campaign encouraged people from the British Commonwealth to move to this country.
- Many people from the West Indies and India moved to Britain. This continued in the 1960s with new immigrants arriving from Asia and Africa.
- During the 1960s race relations laws made it illegal to discriminate against people because of their nationality or race.
- Emigration from Britain to Australia, New Zealand and South Africa was at its height during the 1970s and 1980s.
- By the 1990s Britain's population was around 58 million and 16 per cent of the population were aged 65 or over.

> ### Key Point
>
> The population rose from 47 million to 58 million between 1948 and 1997.

Britain's population growth.

Work Changes

- The world of work has changed a great deal since 1945.
- Traditional industries included coal mining, ship building and steel work.
- These industries have largely disappeared. There is a greater focus now on service industries, banking and finance.
- Between the 1940s and 1990s the number of women in work doubled from 6 million to 12 million.
- In the 1970s goods made in British factories cost more to produce than importing them from overseas.
- This meant that a lot of British factories had to close down and unemployment increased.
- Many coal mines closed because the demand for coal in Britain had declined. Electricity was now generated by power stations burning oil or gas from the North Sea.
- In the 1940s most homes were heated by open coal fires; by the 1980s most homes had central heating powered by gas, oil or electricity.
- In 1972 coal miners went on strike, leading to huge problems in British working life, including the temporary introduction of a three-day working week, so that electricity could be rationed.
- Recently the huge growth in the use of technology has meant that some jobs have relocated overseas.
- Some companies employ people in countries such as India to work in telephone call centres.
- There are now more self-employed people. In 1979 one in twelve workers were self-employed; by the 1990s this had increased to around one in eight.

Key Point
Many traditional industries such as coal mining, shipbuilding and steel work suffered while there was a growth in service industries, banking and finance.

Oil rig.

Workers in an Indian call centre.

> **Quick Test**
>
> 1. Which industries did Labour nationalise after 1945?
> 2. What was the population of Britain by 1997?
> 3. How did immigration help the British economy?
> 4. How many women were in work by the 1990s?
> 5. Why did many coal mines close in the 1970s?

Britain's Place in the World 1945–Present 2

You must be able to:

- Describe reasons why society changed after 1945
- Explain how Britain attempted to rebuild after 1945
- Understand the rise of the teenager and the changing role of women.

Social Change

- There has been huge social and cultural change since the 1940s.
- In the early 1950s few people had a television, and radio was the main form of entertainment. There were plenty of films being made and cinema was very popular.
- Television became more popular following the coronation of the Queen in 1953. Commercial television started in 1955.
- From the 1960s onwards there were huge changes in society.
- Abortion and homosexuality became legal and capital punishment was abolished.
- The contraceptive pill was introduced in the 1960s. At the same time women's roles in society were changing. Many more women could now choose to have a career rather than starting a family and staying at home.
- Young people became known as 'teenagers', and began to break free of parents' control.
- It became acceptable to dress how you wished and listen to new types of music such as rock and roll. British bands such as the Beatles and the Rolling Stones became world famous.
- The voting age was lowered to 18.
- England won the World Cup in 1966, beating West Germany 4–2 at Wembley Stadium.
- By 1963, 82 per cent of all households had a television, 72 per cent a vacuum cleaner, 45 per cent a washing machine and 30 per cent a refrigerator.
- From 1971 to 1983 households having the sole use of a fixed bath or shower rose from 88 per cent to 97 per cent, and those with an indoor toilet from 87 per cent to 97 per cent.
- From 1971 to 1983 the number of households with central heating almost doubled.
- By 1983, 94 per cent of all households had a refrigerator, 81 per cent a colour television, 80 per cent a washing machine, 57 per cent a deep freezer, and 28 per cent a tumble-dryer.
- Popular culture has become a lot richer because of many influences that have come from immigration. West Indian and Asian culture is now part of British life.
- By the beginning of the 21st century, the Internet and social media was changing people's lives.

Key Point

Women and teenagers enjoyed greater freedom and self-expression. Popular culture became a lot richer due to the increase in immigration.

A colour television.

A modern washing machine.

Political and Economic Change

- Britain emerged from the Second World War as one of the top three superpowers, although in reality a distant third behind the USA and the USSR.
- The 1945 Labour government was largely responsible for what is called the 'post-war consensus'.
- There was a belief that the government should play a positive role in ensuring greater equality in a number of ways.
- The government tried to maintain full employment by cutting taxes and increasing spending.
- There was a growing acceptance that trade unions played an important role in protecting workers' rights.
- The government nationalised industries such as gas, electricity, coal and rail.
- The introduction of the NHS and the Welfare State provided free health care for everyone.
- The British Empire was broken up and transformed into the Commonwealth, which was an association of independent states.
- Britain joined the North Atlantic Treaty Organisation (NATO) in 1949 and eventually joined the European Community in 1973.
- During the 1960s and 1970s, successive governments attempted to improve the British economy. Britain's economy was often described as the 'sick man of Europe'.
- The 'Winter of Discontent' in 1979 proved that Britain's economy was struggling.
- There were many strikes in crucial public services.
- The 'Winter of Discontent' turned the public against Labour. The Conservative Party, led by Margaret Thatcher, won the election. She became Britain's first female prime minister.
- During the 1980s the Conservative government privatised many of the nationalised industries, such as gas, electricity and rail.
- The Conservative government remained in power until 1997 when the Labour Party, led by Tony Blair, won the general election using the slogan 'Things can only get better'.
- Britain's relationship with the US and Europe remained important, particularly around the issue of going to war.

> ### Key Point
>
> Britain's place in the world diminished as the two superpowers, the USA and the USSR, grew stronger.

Britain's first female prime minister, Margaret Thatcher.

> ### Timeline
>
> **1945** Labour responsible for post-war consensus.
> **1948** National Health Service introduced.
> **1949** Britain joins NATO.
> **1955** Commercial television begins.
> **1972** Miners' strike.
> **1973** Britain joins the European Community.
> **1979** The Winter of Discontent leads to Labour losing the general election.
> **1979** Margaret Thatcher becomes Britain's first female prime minister.
> **1991** The Internet becomes available to the public.
> **1997** Labour, led by Tony Blair, wins the general election.

> ### Quick Test
>
> 1. What did the introduction of the pill allow women to do?
> 2. How did young people's lives change during the 1950s and 1960s?
> 3. Which two organisations did Britain join and when?
> 4. Why was 1979 known as 'the Winter of Discontent'?
> 5. What was the Labour Party slogan in 1997?

Review Questions

British Transatlantic Slave Trade

Write your answers to the following questions on a separate sheet of paper.

1 Which racist group emerged soon after the Civil War? [1]

2 Which industry thrived in the South? [1]

3 What did Thomas Clarkson and Granville Sharp found? [1]

4 What was the name of the army for the Northern states? [1]

5 Study the source below. It is a painting called *The Old Plantation*, painted by a South Carolina plantation owner, John Rose, around 1785.

What can you learn from this source about life for slaves on plantations?
What are its drawbacks? [5]

6 Describe the difficulties faced by slaves on plantations.

In your answer you should:
- Examine the physical hardships faced by slaves.
- Examine the emotional hardships faced by slaves. [10]

Britain as the First Industrial Nation

Write your answers to the following questions on a separate sheet of paper.

1 How many major cholera epidemics were there in 19th-century London? [1]

2 Who devised Germ Theory? [1]

3 How old were some of the youngest factory workers? [1]

4 What happened in 1853? [1]

5 Study the source below about the spread of cholera. It is a political cartoon from 1866, showing death serving cholera to London's children at a water pump.

What does the source tell you about public knowledge of cholera in 1866? [5]

6 Explain the importance of Germ Theory.

In your answer you should:
- Explain the problems caused by infectious disease.
- Analyse the acceleration of reforms following Germ Theory.
- Suggest what improvements it made to understanding Snow's work. [10]

Review Questions

Democratic Reform

1 Which three cities had no MPs in the 1820s?

.... [1]

2 How many miners and ironworkers took part in the Newport Rising?

.... [1]

3 Who was Prime Minister in 1867?

.... [1]

4 What did the 1874 Factory Act allow workers to do?

.... [1]

5 In your opinion, why was the 1884 Parliamentary Reform Act an important development?

In your answer you should:
- Give at least two examples of changes to the voting system in 1884.
- Use facts to support your answer.

Write your answer on a separate sheet of paper. [10]

6 Study the source below on the Newport Rising in November 1839.

> A company of soldiers was stationed at the Westgate Hotel. The crowd marched there, loudly cheering. The police fled into the hotel for safety. The soldiers were stationed at the windows, through which some of the crowd fired. The soldiers returned the fire. In about twenty minutes ten of the Chartists were killed on the spot, and fifty others wounded.

What does this source tell you about the Newport Rising that would help you write an account of the event? What are its drawbacks?

Give reasons for your answer.

Write your answer on a separate sheet of paper. [5]

Women's Suffrage

1 In what year did the women's movements start to differ over the methods used?

_____ [1]

2 How many women went to Downing Street to protest in 1906?

_____ [1]

3 Which three buildings were the main targets of violence in 1911?

_____ [1]

4 Why did the government introduce a new voting law during the First World War?

_____ [1]

5 Describe how the Cat and Mouse Act gained sympathy for the Suffragette movement.

In your answer you should:
- Explain at least three examples.
- Use facts to support your answer.

Write your answer on a separate sheet of paper. [10]

6 Study the source below, which is from the Speaker of the House of Commons in 1913.

> The activities of the suffragettes had reached a stage at which nothing was safe from attacks. Churches were burnt, buildings and houses were destroyed, bombs were exploded, the police assaulted and meetings broken up. The feelings in the House hardened opposition to their demands. The result was a defeat of their Bill by 47 votes, which the government had previously promised to support.

Explain why the government failed to support the Suffragette movement.

Write your answer on a separate sheet of paper. [5]

The First World War

1 In what month and year did the First World War break out?

_____ [1]

2 What infection affected soldiers' feet in the trenches?

_____ [1]

3 Which general led the French forces at the Battle of Verdun?

_____ [1]

4 Where did the main battle between forces from the British Empire and Turkey occur in 1915?

_____ [1]

5 In your opinion, what was the main cause of the First World War?

In your answer you should:
- Give your opinion of the most important cause.
- Compare your opinion to at least two other causes.

Write your answer on a separate sheet of paper. [10]

6 Describe why the Battle of the Somme is often viewed as a disaster for the British.

In your answer you should:
- Explain at least three different negative outcomes for the British.
- Use facts and figures to support your answer.

Write your answer on a separate sheet of paper. [10]

The Second World War

1 Why did Hitler want to invade the Rhineland in 1936?

_____ [1]

2 How did Neville Chamberlain try to prevent war?

_____ [1]

3 What did the Nazi–Soviet Pact agree upon?

_____ [1]

4 Why did Hitler want to invade the USSR?

_____ [1]

5 Describe the ways in which people were persecuted during the Holocaust.

In your answer you should:
- Give at least three different examples.
- Use facts to support your answer.

Write your answer on a separate sheet of paper. [10]

6 Describe why the Battle of Britain was a success for Britain.

In your answer you should:
- Explain at least three negative outcomes for Hitler.
- Use facts to support your answer.

Write your answer on a separate sheet of paper. [10]

The Creation of the Welfare State

1 Which party emerged as the 'voice of the working class'?

.... [1]

2 Which war highlighted the poor health of possible recruits?

.... [1]

3 A thousand of what were built to deal with the effects of the air raids?

.... [1]

4 When was the NHS established?

.... [1]

5 Explain the reasons for the programme of Liberal welfare reforms.

In your answer you should:
- Give your opinion of the most important cause.
- Give details of at least three motivations for reform.

Write your answer on a separate sheet of paper. [10]

6 How did the war years (1939–45) create a need for new welfare reforms?

In your answer you should:
- Explain the problems highlighted by the war.
- Describe extra services provided because of the war.
- Outline the impact of the Beveridge Report.

Write your answer on a separate sheet of paper. [10]

Britain's Place in the World 1945–Present

1 In what year did food rationing end?

_____ [1]

2 Which three countries did British people emigrate to?

_____ [1]

3 In what year did commercial television begin?

_____ [1]

4 What problem occurred due to the 1972 miners' strike?

_____ [1]

5 In your opinion, what is the most important change in Britain since 1945 (for example, social, political, industrial)?

In your answer you should:
- Give your opinion on the most important change.
- Compare your opinions on at least two examples of change.

Write your answer on a separate sheet of paper. [10]

6 Describe why the 1960s changed the lives of women and teenagers.

In your answer you should:
- Describe at least three different positive outcomes.
- Use facts and figures to support your answer.

Write your answer on a separate sheet of paper. [10]

Migration To and From the British Isles 1

You must be able to:

- Describe historical trends of immigration to Britain
- Understand why there was mass immigration to Britain post Second World War
- Explain why immigration legislation arose in the 1960s and 1970s.

Immigration to Britain

- In the 3rd century a group of African men were brought to Britain to guard Hadrian's Wall.
- A Jewish population was recorded in the 12th century.
- By 1770, there were 14 000 black people in Britain as a result of the slave trade but few had any real freedom.
- During the First World War, 60 000 seamen were drafted in from the British Empire, as well as many soldiers. Some remained in Britain during the interwar years. However they faced a great deal of prejudice and there were riots against black settlers in 1919.
- Following the Second World War Britain started to become a more multicultural nation.

> ### Key Point
>
> These are just some examples of minority groups within Britain. There have been many immigrant groups arriving at various points in Britain's history.

After the Second World War

- Many British politicians spoke proudly of Britain's fight against the racism of Nazi Germany and insisted Britain was different.
- At this point there were relatively few black or Asian people living in Britain.
- Many soldiers from the Commonwealth had fought for Britain during the war.
- The 1948 British Nationality Act gave all 800 million people of the Commonwealth the right to claim British citizenship.
- Immigration from the Commonwealth was not restricted until 1962.
- From 1955 to 1961, approximately 30 000 people a year were emigrating from the Commonwealth to Britain.

A British passport.

Why was Immigration so High?

- The main reason for high immigration after the Second World War was that Britain had a shortage of workers. The NHS had been established in 1948 and desperately needed more workers.
- London Transport went to the Caribbean to recruit workers.
- Working in Britain was seen as an opportunity to earn a good wage, some of which workers could send back to their families.
- Incentives such as interest-free loans to cover transport costs and the cost of setting up a new home in Britain were offered.

Problems with Immigration

- Racial tensions soon began to develop in communities.
- Highly skilled immigrants were given unskilled jobs.
- Living conditions for immigrants were often cramped.
- Language barriers made it hard for some to find work.
- Newspapers published sensationalist headlines about unclean behaviour and criminal activity among immigrants.
- Young white men sometimes attacked immigrants as there was jealousy over women.

The Notting Hill Riots 1958

- A large Caribbean community lived in Notting Hill.
- Groups of young white men armed themselves with knives and petrol bombs and attacked the black community.
- Over 100 people were arrested.

New Legislation

Law	Details of the Law
Commonwealth Immigration Act 1962.	Migrants must have a prearranged job before they can come to Britain and to have been issued with an employment voucher.
The Race Relations Act 1965 and 1968.	Discrimination in employment and housing banned. Incitement of racial hatred illegal.
Commonwealth Immigrants Act 1968.	As well as an employment voucher they must also have a parent or grandparent in the UK.
Immigration Act 1971.	Replaced employment vouchers with 12-month work permits.

> **Key Point**
>
> Immigration remains a controversial and key political issue today.

The annual Notting Hill Carnival takes place to promote cultural unity.

Quick Test

1. Why did the Romans bring Africans to Britain?
2. By 1770, how many black people were in the UK?
3. Name a company trying to recruit workers after the Second World War.
4. What sort of stories did newspapers publish about immigrants?
5. Where were there riots in 1958?

Migration To and From the British Isles 2

You must be able to:

- Understand that many people have emigrated from Britain as well as immigrating to it
- Understand why certain groups left Britain
- Explain the problems they faced when arriving in a new country.

Emigration from Britain

- Emigration from Britain is not new.
- The Pilgrim Fathers, groups of Scottish people and many Irish people emigrated as a result of persecution and extreme hardship.

The Pilgrim Fathers

- During the reign of Elizabeth I, England was Protestant.
- However, a small group of Puritans (members of a strict Protestant movement) felt they were being persecuted in England because of their beliefs.
- At first they left for Holland but remained unhappy there.
- In the summer of 1620, 120 of these Puritans set sail for Virginia where they could set up their own community.
- They were taking a huge risk as they only had a small boat, and others before them had tried and failed to adapt to life in Virginia.
- They faced a difficult journey on their ship, the *Mayflower*, and got blown much further than Virginia.
- They arrived in November, having travelled for three months.
- Most were suffering from scurvy, due to a lack of Vitamin C, by the time they arrived.
- Most of the Native Americans were dead at this point having caught smallpox from previous European settlers.
- The Pilgrim Fathers took food from offerings on Native American graves and used their abandoned homes.
- Some remaining Native Americans attacked them, but were driven away by the Pilgrim Fathers' guns.
- Half of the Pilgrim Fathers died in the first winter. Those who survived did so because they had befriended some of the Native Americans, who helped them build homes and learn to find food in their new environment.
- The end of a successful harvest in 1621 was marked with a special meal, which is what Americans now remember at Thanksgiving.
- More Puritans left England to join this new community. By 1640, 20 000 had arrived and the city of Boston was created.

Key Point

By the end of the 19th century, 5 million British lived outside of Britain.

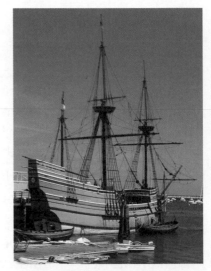

A replica of the *Mayflower*.

A replica of a settlement created by the Pilgrim Fathers.

Canadian Scots

- By the 18th century the British Empire was huge, but many parts were of little use because of their small populations.
- The British government sold a large piece of Canadian land, Nova Scotia or 'New Scotland', to two Scottish businessmen.
- They encouraged many Scottish families to go and work for them in 1773.
- The journey was long and difficult. Eighteen children died of dysentery or smallpox on the first ship sent there, *The Hector*.
- When they arrived the work was hard, but they developed a thriving timber industry which then exported to Britain.
- By the end of the 19th century, there were over 250 000 Scottish people in Canada.

The Irish Potato Famine

- In the 19th century there was mass emigration from Ireland, then part of Britain, due to extreme hardship.
- Most Irish farmers were poor and lived off a simple diet with potato being the staple food.
- This led to disaster when, in 1845, the harvest failed due to potato blight.
- By 1849, 1 million people had died, either from starvation or related illnesses.
- Over 4 million Irish people emigrated, mostly to the USA.
- In addition, 150 000 settled in England, mainly in Liverpool and Manchester.
- Those who chose to go to America faced a long and expensive journey.
- A ticket was around £200 in today's money and only bought a bed in a cramped cabin with poor facilities.
- Most families struggled to find that money, so often one family member would go and send money back to Ireland.
- Upon arrival in America they faced medical inspections at the notorious Ellis Island.
- Anyone found unfit for work was immediately sent back.
- Life was not easy in America. The Irish migrants often found themselves living in poor tenement blocks and being stigmatised for their Catholic beliefs.

Quick Test

1. What form of religion did the Pilgrim Fathers practise?
2. What city did they found?
3. Which diseases killed a lot of Scots en route to Canada?
4. What crop failed in Ireland?
5. How much was a ticket to America in the 1840s?

The Nova Scotia flag.

Key Point

In all three case studies the journey was very difficult.

Ellis Island in New York.

Timeline

1620 Pilgrim Fathers arrive in America.
1773 Scots arrive in Canada.
1840s Many Irish leave for America.
1948 British Nationality Act.
1962 Commonwealth Immigration Act in Britain.
1965 and 1968 Race Relations Act in Britain.
1968 Commonwealth Immigrants Act in Britain.
1971 Immigration Act in Britain.

USA in the 20th Century 1

You must be able to:

- Explain the growth of the economy
- Describe why prohibition failed
- Understand why the Wall Street Crash happened.

Economic Growth in the 1920s

- This decade was a period of prosperity: incomes rose and standards of living improved.
- The stock market boomed and many people bought shares.
- The motor industry boomed as cars became more affordable. Ford, Chrysler and General Motors all became huge companies.
- The Model T Ford cost less than $300.
- More people could afford to buy items such as fridges, radios, washing machines and vacuum cleaners.

A 1920s Ford car.

Poverty in the 1920s

- Despite the boom in the economy there was still poverty. Wealth was not distributed evenly and there was a big gap between rich and poor.
- Many people had moved to the cities in order to find work, but many of these jobs were poorly paid.
- Old industries such as coal mining suffered hugely and the railways suffered due to the increase in car production.
- Farmers had benefitted during the First World War, but now began to suffer. They grew more food than was needed and this led to falling prices and less profit.
- 25 per cent of the wealth in the USA was owned by the richest 5 per cent of people.

> **Key Point**
>
> There were winners and losers during the 1920s, even though this was seen as a time of prosperity.

Discrimination

- There was prejudice towards immigrant groups during the 1920s.
- Many African-Americans had moved from the Southern states to the North in search of work but they were poorly treated and often discriminated against.
- In 1924 a National Origins Act was introduced which placed strict limits on immigration.
- The Ku Klux Klan (KKK) had been formed in the 1860s and gained further popularity during the 1920s. Membership had risen to approximately 4 million by 1925.

A member of the KKK.

Prohibition

- In 1920 it became illegal to manufacture, produce or distribute alcohol. This was called prohibition.
- Temperance movements believed that alcohol led to violence, immoral behaviour and the breakdown of family life.
- Businessmen blamed alcohol for making workers lazy and unreliable and the middle classes believed alcohol caused social problems among immigrant workers.
- Bars and saloons were closed down and the US authorities recruited over 1500 agents to enforce prohibition.
- In response, illegal bars, called speakeasies, were set up.

The production of alcohol, such as whisky, became illegal.

Organised Crime

- Prohibition saw a huge rise in organised crime as rival gangs fought to control the business and make millions of dollars.
- Al Capone made $60 million per year from alcohol. He used a private army to run his business and fight rival gangs, but was eventually arrested for tax evasion in 1931.
- The St Valentine's Day Massacre of 1929, organised by Al Capone against a rival gang, is the most famous incidence of gang violence.
- Prohibition had proved almost impossible to enforce and there was widespread corruption. It ended in 1933.

> ## Key Point
>
> Prohibition failed because the demand for alcohol continued. Criminals moved in to supply alcohol, made huge profits and developed sophisticated criminal networks.

The Wall Street Crash

- On 24 October 1929 approximately 13 million shares were sold, but confidence in the value of these shares plummeted.
- Loss of confidence led to falling prices and this meant losses of stock for brokers and private investors. This increased pressure on the banks to help people out.
- Once share prices began to fall, many people panicked and tried to sell or withdraw their savings from the banks. This caused many banks to go bust.
- The US economy suffered a depression and there was terrible poverty in the years that followed. Confidence in the economy had been destroyed.
- In 1932, approximately 20 000 businesses and 5 000 banks were forced to close.

> ## Key Point
>
> The Wall Street Crash had a devastating effect on the US economy, which took years to fully recover.

A sign for Wall Street in New York City.

> ## Quick Test
>
> 1. How much did a Model T Ford cost in the 1920s?
> 2. Which industries suffered in the 1920s?
> 3. What is a speakeasy?
> 4. What year did prohibition become law?
> 5. How many shares were sold on 24 October 1929?

USA in the 20th Century 2

You must be able to:

- Explain how the Cold War developed
- Describe why the USA fought the Vietnam war
- Understand the methods used to gain civil rights.

The Cold War

- After the Second World War, the USA and USSR were the world's major superpowers.
- Both nations were very competitive, but also felt threatened by each other's power.
- An arms race developed to have the most powerful weapons, in particular nuclear weapons.
- This increasing tension was known as the Cold War. This is because there wasn't actually any fighting, just fear and suspicion of each other.
- Countries in Western Europe tended to support the USA and most countries in Eastern Europe were dominated by the power of the USSR.
- Both sides were afraid of another war because of the potential use of nuclear weapons.
- People thought it would be the end of the world if a nuclear war between the USA and USSR broke out.

Vietnam

- Vietnam had become independent from France in the 1950s and was split in two. North Vietnam became Communist and South Vietnam had an anti-Communist government.
- This alarmed the USA because it was concerned about the spread of Communism in Asia.
- President Kennedy sent financial aid and military equipment to support the South Vietnamese.
- In 1964, US ships were attacked by the North Vietnamese and this led to full-scale war.
- In 1965, there were 125 000 US soldiers fighting in Vietnam. This had increased to 500 000 by 1968.
- The US found it very difficult to fight in the jungles of Vietnam. It used tactics such as heavy bombing and chemical weapons to try to defeat the Vietnamese.
- In 1968 the North Vietnamese launched an all-out attack known as the Tet Offensive. This took the US by surprise and they suffered heavy losses.

Nuclear weapons.

> ### Key Point
>
> The war had become increasingly unpopular and expensive to finance. It had dragged on for years and many soldiers had died. Many Americans felt that the war had been an embarrassment.

An artist's impression of two fighter bombers over South Vietnam.

- By August 1968 the Tet Offensive was over and both sides had suffered heavy casualties.
- Initial peace talks held in 1968 were unsuccessful. North Vietnam refused to withdraw its troops from South Vietnam.
- In 1973, peace was agreed at the Paris Peace Conference.
- The President of South Vietnam would stay in power. The North Vietnamese could keep areas of land that it already controlled.
- All US prisoners of war were to be released.
- All US troops were to leave within two months.

Civil Rights

- Despite being freed from slavery in 1860, African-Americans in the US were still poorly treated and discriminated against in the 20th century.
- Segregation of theatres, schools, restaurants, workplaces, toilets and public transport in the South was enforced by law.
- In 1955 in Montgomery, Alabama, Rosa Parks refused to give up her seat on a bus for a white man. She was arrested.
- Protests were led by Martin Luther King and a bus boycott took place.
- Non-violent protest won support from people. Peaceful protests, sit-ins and marches helped to gain publicity and sympathy for the cause. African-Americans demanded to be treated equally in the law.
- In 1963, 250 000 people marched on Washington to demand civil rights. This is where Martin Luther King made his famous 'I have a dream' speech.
- In 1964, the Civil Rights Act was passed. This gave the government the power to end segregation in all public places.
- In the South there were lots of local laws in place designed to stop African-Americans from voting.
- In 1965, the Voting Rights Act was passed and this meant that voting rights could be legally enforced.
- Martin Luther King's call for peaceful protest and non-violent methods was vitally important in the struggle for civil rights.
- However there were groups who believed that non-violent protest was too slow. They believed in Black Power.
- Malcolm X, The Nation of Islam, and the Black Panthers all favoured direct action.

> **Key Point**
>
> The civil rights movement eventually gained the equality and freedom that was demanded. Although different methods were used, Martin Luther King is widely recognised as playing a vital role with his methods of peaceful protest.

Memorial statue of Martin Luther King.

> **Timeline**
>
> **1920** Prohibition introduced.
> **1929** The Wall Street Crash.
> **1929** St Valentine's Day Massacre.
> **1931** Al Capone arrested.
> **1933** Prohibition ended.
> **1945** End of Second World War.
> **1955** Rosa Parks and the bus boycott.
> **1963** Martin Luther King delivers his 'I have a dream' speech.
> **1964** Civil Rights Act passed in USA.
> **1968** 500 000 soldiers fighting in Vietnam.

> **Quick Test**
>
> 1. Who supported the USA during the Cold War?
> 2. What weapons were the USA and Russia trying to build up?
> 3. How many soldiers were in Vietnam in 1965?
> 4. Where did Martin Luther King deliver his famous speech?
> 5. In what year was the Voting Rights Act passed?

Review Questions

The Creation of the Welfare State

1 What did Chadwick make a link between?

_____ [1]

2 Which country was a major industrial power and had a good welfare system at the beginning of the 20th century?

_____ [1]

3 In 1908, what was the life expectancy of most workers?

_____ [1]

4 Whose throats did Bevan 'stuff with gold'?

_____ [1]

5 Study the source below, which is a quote from Dr John Marks, who qualified as a doctor on the day the NHS was established.

> Doctors were a pretty conservative bunch, certainly the older ones, and many hated the NHS. They saw it as the government interfering in the doctor and patient relationship, although some just opposed it outright on political grounds.

What can you learn from this source about why doctors opposed the NHS? What does it not tell you?

Write your answer on a separate sheet of paper. [5]

6 What were the limitations of the programme of Liberal welfare reforms?

In your answer you should:
- Use facts and figures to support your answer.
- Give your opinion about what the main limitations were.

Write your answer on a separate sheet of paper. [10]

Britain's Place in the World 1945–Present

1 In what year did the Suez Crisis take place?

.... [1]

2 Which two countries were regarded as world superpowers?

.... [1]

3 Name the two most popular pop music bands in the 1960s.

.... [1]

4 What percentage of people owned a television by 1963?

.... [1]

5 Describe the changes in work since 1945.

In your answer you should:
- Give your opinion on the most important changes.
- Compare your opinion on at least two examples of change.

Write your answer on a separate sheet of paper. [10]

6 Describe the reasons why the British population grew between 1948 and 1997.

In your answer you should:
- Explain at least three different outcomes.
- Use facts and figures to support your answer.

Write your answer on a separate sheet of paper. [10]

Migration To and From the British Isles

Write your answers to the following questions on a separate sheet of paper.

1 When was a Jewish population first recorded in Britain? [1]

2 What was the main occupation of black people in Britain in the Middle Ages? [1]

3 What did Thanksgiving originally celebrate? [1]

4 What did young white men often accuse black immigrants of doing? [1]

5 Study the source below. It shows racist graffiti in London in the 1950s.

Why does this source **not** give you enough information about the problems black immigrants faced in Britain in the 1950s? [5]

6 Describe immigration to Britain prior to the Second World War.

In your answer you should mention:
* Pre-First World War immigration.
* Immigration as a result of the First World War. [10]

USA in the 20th Century

Write your answers to the following questions on a separate sheet of paper.

1 In what year was the National Origins Act introduced? [1]

2 How many members of the Ku Klux Klan (KKK) were there by 1925? [1]

3 In 1932, how many banks were forced to close? [1]

4 In what year did slavery end? [1]

5 In your opinion, why did organised crime increase so rapidly during the 1920s?

In your answer you should:
- Give your opinion on at least three examples.
- Use facts and figures to support your answer. [10]

6 Study the source below, which is a cartoon from 1962 showing the leaders of the USSR and the USA arm wrestling.

Describe how useful the source is for understanding the Cold War. What are its drawbacks? [5]

History – Six Key Skills

Chronological understanding

- This is where you try to gain an understanding of dates and the time period you're studying.
- An example could be, what was it like to live in the Middle Ages?

Cultural, ethnic and religious diversity

- This is where you try to understand how different people would have different experiences in the same time period.
- An example could be, how would a landowner's experience of the Peasants' Revolt be different from a peasant's experience?

Change and continuity

- This is where you identify any factors that have changed or continued over a period of time.
- An example could be, how did a king's power change between 1066 and 1660?

Cause and consequence

- This is where you try to explain the reasons for an event happening and the impact the event has.
- An example could be, what were the reasons (causes) for the First World War and what was its impact (consequences)?

Significance

- This is where you try to explain why something is important.
- An example could be, why was the Industrial Revolution so important (significant) to Britain?

Interpretation

- This is when you try to explain why some people think differently about the same event.
- An example could be, why might a Norman think differently about the Norman Conquest compared to a Saxon?

> **Key Point**

The more often you include these skills in your work the better your work will be and the quicker you will progress!

Answers

Pages 4–19 Revise Questions

Page 5 Quick Test: The Norman Conquest 1
1. 1066
2. Harold
3. Edward the Confessor
4. Bayeux Tapestry
5. The feudal system

Page 7 Quick Test: The Norman Conquest 2
1. Northern England and eastern England (the Fens)
2. Hereward the Wake
3. A motte
4. Domesday Book
5. 1087

Page 9 Quick Test: Christendom and the Crusades 1
1. The Pope
2. The Archbishop of Canterbury
3. Monks and nuns (abbots, abbesses and friars also acceptable answers)
4. You were no longer a member of the Catholic Church and were damned according to the Catholic authorities
5. To help them get into heaven

Page 11 Quick Test: Christendom and the Crusades 2
1. Thomas A'Becket
2. 1170
3. To escape punishment
4. A Muslim warrior and king
5. King Richard I

Page 13 Quick Test: Magna Carta 1
1. John soft sword
2. Stephen Langton
3. Stopped marriages and burials in England and excommunicated him
4. Took money from the Church and expelled monks from England
5. Great Charter

Page 15 Quick Test: Magna Carta 2
1. 1215
2. Runnymede
3. £100
4. Barons and bishops
5. Knights and townspeople

Page 17 Quick Test: The Black Death 1
1. 1348–50
2. The Middle East
3. From fleas that lived on rats
4. 200 million
5. Toads and leeches

Page 19 Quick Test: The Black Death 2
1. Flu symptoms, sweating, coughing, lumps on arms and legs (first red, then black), high temperature, blotches
2. Five days
3. Jewish people
4. Food prices rose
5. Villeins were given more food and money for working the land

Pages 20–21 Review Questions

Key Stage 2 Topics

1. The correct order is C, A, E, B, D (Iron Age hill forts were built in Britain in 550 BC; the Roman invasion of Britain by Claudius was in AD 43; Boudicca's uprising against the Romans was in AD 61; Augustine's mission sets up Christianity in Britain in 597 AD; Alfred the Great ruled England from AD 871 to AD 899) [5]

2. Julius Caesar was a **Roman** general. He invaded Britain in 55 BCE, which stands for **Before** the Common Era. Alfred the Great was an **Anglo-Saxon** king. He created peace between the Vikings and the English.

   St Cuthbert was a Christian monk. He brought Christianity to northern England.

   He built a big monastery on an island off the east coast of northern England called **Lindisfarne**. [5]

3. There is no one right answer to this question; you can select any individual but you must give a reason. For example: Julius Caesar because he was powerful enough to invade England; Alfred the Great because he secured peace and order between the Vikings and the English; St Cuthbert, because he spread Christianity throughout the country. [2]

4. There is no one right answer to this question; you can select any individual but you must give a reason. For example, Julius Caesar because although he invaded Britain, lots of other individuals did too; Alfred the Great

because he did not bring anything to Britain; St Cuthbert because he only spread Christianity in the northern part of England. [2]

5. a. Conditions were poor – dangerous, scary, worrying, cruel, violent. [3]

   b. Source A talks about the negative points of working in a factory [1], while Source B talks about the positive aspects of working in a factory [1]. For example, Source A mentions the dangers such as loss of fingers [1] while Source B describes some good things the children received such as education [1]. [2 marks for an understanding of both sources, plus 2 marks for an example from both sources.]

   c. One mark for each of the following, up to a maximum of 3 marks: To get more people to work in his factory; to make sure his factory didn't get closed down; to make sure he kept receiving money; to show how conditions had improved after the 1833 Factory Act. [3]

6. a. They have labels and are carrying suitcases and bags. [2]

   b. i. Mothers would be upset and lonely because it meant splitting up their family. [2]

      ii. Children would be upset, lonely, and/or excited. They would miss their family and might forget their parents. [2]

      iii. There would be lots of adults and no children. Schools might close down. [2]

Pages 22–25 Practice Questions

Page 22 The Norman Conquest

1. Germany [1]
2. Normandy [1]
3. Harald Hardrada [1]
4. An outer area around Norman castles containing housing and surrounded by a fence [1]

For questions 5 and 6, see Mark Scheme A.

5. Your answer should include the following reasons, backed up with explanations and facts:
   * William was a relation of the Saxon king, Edward the Confessor.
   * Harold, King of the Saxons, was proclaimed English king on the death of Edward the Confessor.
   * William was one of a number of foreign monarchs who could claim the English throne.

6. A good answer would include the following reasons:
   * The Saxons had already fought at Stamford Bridge and would therefore have been tired.
   * The Saxon's king, Harold, had been killed meaning they did not have a leader.
   * William's army did not have as far to walk so they were in better fighting spirit than the Saxons.

Page 23 Christendom and the Crusades

1. Emperor of Byzantium [1]
2. Canterbury [1]
3. Jerusalem [1]
4. A journey to a religious place [1]

For questions 5 and 6 see Mark Scheme A.

5. There is no right answer to this question and you need to use your imagination. You might include the following points:
   * You cannot read or write so you look to Church leaders, like priests, for guidance and help.
   * Monasteries provide you with shelter and food when going on a pilgrimage and offer help when you are sick or orphaned.
   * You believe life on earth is short, after you die you will go to heaven or hell, and religion can help you get to heaven.

6. Here are some of the differences you might mention in your answer:
   * Priests were educated and could read and write. They looked after a parish of people, usually in a village. They worked among ordinary people and conducted daily religious services for them.
   * Monks lived in monasteries separate from ordinary people. They did not conduct religious services for ordinary people, but they performed a variety of functions such as praying for people to get to heaven and looking after the sick, elderly and needy.

Page 24 Magna Carta

1. 1215 [1]
2. The powers of the English king [1]
3. Trial by jury of fellow Englishmen [1]
4. Excommunicated him [1]

For questions 5 and 6 see Mark Scheme A.

5. A good answer would make the following points:
   * John was not a warrior like his predecessor, his elder brother, Richard the Lionheart.
   * John lost lands in France.
   * He quarrelled with the Pope and the Church.
   * He fought and lost a war with the barons.
   * John was forced to sign Magna Carta.

6. A good answer would include the following reasons:
   * John had lost wars in France.
   * He conducted costly wars in Ireland and Scotland, which cost the barons money.
   * John did not consult the barons in the running of the country.
   * John had a major quarrel with the Church and the Pope, which affected the barons.

Page 25 The Black Death

1. 7500 [1]
2. The lumps on the body turned black [1]

3. Roughly every 10 years [1]
4. Due to a labour shortage, they were offered more money and land to work the lord's land [1]

For questions 5 and 6 see Mark Scheme A.

5. A good answer would include the following reasons:
   - Description of two symptoms such as sweating, coughing, buboes, high temperatures or blotches.
   - Explanation of the problems these would cause.
   - The Black Death mainly led to the victims dying within five days.

6. A good answer would include some of the following methods:
   - By praying and punishing themselves because they believed the Black Death had been sent by God.
   - Blaming and attacking foreigners for bringing the disease to England.
   - Moving out of towns and places where the Black Death occurred.
   - Using a variety of remedies to stop them contracting the disease, such as herbs, flowers, fire and animals.

Pages 26–41 Revise Questions

Page 27 Quick Test: The Peasants' Revolt 1
1. Introduction of the Poll Tax in 1380
2. Essex and Kent (counties close to London)
3. 10 years old
4. Five pence
5. Fobbing

Page 29 Quick Test: The Peasants' Revolt 2
1. Wat Tyler
2. Mile End
3. Ending the Poll Tax, freedom for all, and that the poor should receive the Church's wealth
4. Ending the Poll Tax
5. Rioting

Page 31 Quick Test: Reformation and Counter Reformation 1
1. Latin
2. Germany
3. Because he did not have a son and Catherine was too old to have any more children
4. Anne Boleyn
5. 1536

Page 33 Quick Test: Reformation and Counter Reformation 2
1. 1539
2. Edward Seymour
3. English
4. The bread and wine were symbolic and did not actually become the body and blood of Jesus
5. She put to death many of the Catholic Church's opponents

Page 35 Quick Test: The English Civil Wars 1
1. She was Catholic
2. A new prayer book

3. His nephew Prince Rupert
4. The Battle of Edgehill
5. The Battle of Marston Moor

Page 37 Quick Test: The English Civil Wars 2
1. The New Model Army
2. Bristol
3. The Scots
4. He only chose those he knew wanted the King to stand trial
5. 30 January 1649

Page 39 Quick Test: The Interregnum 1
1. The King had been executed
2. Oliver Cromwell selected 140 Puritans to become MPs
3. Its MPs had extreme views and they wanted to change the theft law
4. Executive powers as Lord Protector
5. They were responsible for tax collection, law enforcement, and preventing opposition

Page 41 Quick Test: The Interregnum 2
1. Theatres, pubs and dancing
2. He had imposed strict rules and raised taxes
3. He was concerned that people would question his motives
4. He did not have the support of the army and Parliament
5. He got rid of the Puritans' harsh laws

Pages 42–45 Review Questions

Page 42 The Norman Conquest
1. Middle Ages [1]
2. The king [1]
3. Farm labourers or peasants who had to work several days each year for their lord in return for small plots of land [1]
4. In the decade after 1066 [1]

For questions 5 and 6 see Mark Scheme A.

5. Your answer should include the following difficulties faced by Harold, backed up with full explanations:
   - He had to march his army to Yorkshire to fight Harald Hardrada, King of Norway and Denmark, in the north of England in 1066.
   - He then had to march his army all the way to Sussex to fight William of Normandy shortly afterwards.

6. Your answer should include the following ways in which castles helped William control England, backed up with explanations and facts:
   - Castles became local centres of military power.
   - They allowed the Normans to control England.
   - Castles were a symbol of Norman power.

Page 43 Christendom and the Crusades
1. 1170 [1]
2. Byzantium [1]

3. Monasteries [1]
4. Salah u Din, also known as Saladin [1]

For questions 5 and 6 see Mark Scheme A.

5. A good answer might make the following points:
   - People were very religious in the Middle Ages.
   - It was believed that good people who did good things would have eternal life in heaven.
   - Those who behaved badly on earth would face eternal pain and suffering in hell.

6. Students' answers must link back to religious reasons. A good answer would fully describe and explain the following:
   - To capture Jerusalem because it was of religious importance.
   - To enter into heaven.
   - To increase the power of the Church.

Page 44 Magna Carta

1. Poitou [1]
2. Villeins (those not freemen) [1]
3. The barons and bishops [1]
4. In 1265 by Simon de Montfort [1]

For questions 5 and 6 see Mark Scheme A.

5. A good answer would include the following:
   - The King had to consult the barons.
   - The King eventually had to call a Parliament in order to raise taxes.
   - The King had limited power in his dealings with the Church.
   - Freemen now had the right to trial by jury.

6. There is no right answer to this question; you need to use your imagination. Some points you might make are:
   - John had a major quarrel with the Pope and Church, which meant religious services were withdrawn and churches shut down.
   - John lost lots of land in France.
   - John fought costly wars in Ireland and against Scotland.
   - John gave freemen rights under Magna Carta.
   - Many of John's problems were caused by the barons.

Page 45 The Black Death

1. By boat from the Middle East [1]
2. Figs and butter [1]
3. The populations had declined so severely [1]
4. Tried to keep wages at pre-Black Death levels [1]

For questions 5 and 6 see Mark Scheme A.

5. A good answer would cover the following points, backed up with evidence and full explanations:
   - Villages were abandoned.
   - There was a shortage of labour.
   - Many people began to lose faith in religion.
   - It helped create the conditions for the Peasants' Revolt.

6. There is no right answer to this question; you need to use your imagination. Try to capture the fear and panic that the Black Death caused. You might include some of the following issues:
   - Fear that the end of the world was coming.
   - Fear that the Black Death was a punishment from God.
   - The need to flee areas affected by the disease, leaving behind your source of work.
   - If you were a foreigner you might be blamed and attacked for bringing the disease to England.

Pages 46–49 **Practice Questions**

Page 46 The Peasants' Revolt

1. A shortage of villeins [1]
2. Simon of Sudbury and Robert Hales [1]
3. 116 years [1]
4. John Ball [1]

For questions 5 and 6 see Mark Scheme A.

5. Whatever your opinion, a good answer would include some of the following considerations:
   - Richard II was very young and had to rely on others to help him make decisions.
   - He inherited a costly war with France.
   - He unwisely introduced the Poll Tax, which treated rich and poor alike.
   - He helped cause the Peasants' Revolt.

6. A good answer would include the following causes:
   - The Black Death had led to a major drop in the population and villeins no longer wanted to work without wages.
   - The Poll Tax treated rich and poor alike and this was resented by the poor.
   - Richard II was fighting a very costly war with France for which he kept raising taxes.
   - Peasants believed Richard II was badly advised and wanted an end to the Poll Tax.
   - A judgement on the most important cause should be reached.

Page 47 Reformation and Counter Reformation

1. The Act of Supremacy 1534 [1]
2. Over 800 [1]
3. Philip of Spain [1]
4. Over 200 [1]

For questions 5 and 6 see Mark Scheme A.

5. A good answer would fully describe and explain the following:
   - Henry VIII wanted to divorce Catherine of Aragon. The Pope refused to allow him so he had to break with Rome.
   - Henry VIII wanted more wealth, which he wanted to take from the Church.
   - Henry VIII wanted more power. By being Head of the Church he became very powerful.

- Ideas about forming a Christian Church outside the Catholic Church were gaining popularity in England at the time of Henry VIII's reign.
6. A good answer would fully describe and explain the following:
   - Henry VIII was now seen as Head of the Church, not the Pope.
   - Religious services were in English instead of Latin.
   - Bibles in English were placed in every church.
   - Church services were made simpler.

Page 48 The English Civil War

1. The years 1629–40 when Charles I ruled without Parliament [1]
2. August 1642 [1]
3. The Battle of Edgehill [1]
4. Outside the Banqueting Hall in London [1]

For questions 5 and 6 see Mark Scheme A.

5. Your answer should give an opinion and compare it to two others. Possible causes are:
   - Religion
   - Power
   - Money.
6. Your answer might include the following reasons, with the best answers making comparisons to other battles.
   - After this battle it became clear the Royalists would lose the war.
   - Cromwell rose to lead the Parliamentarians during this battle.
   - This battle was a decisive victory, unlike Edgehill where no one won.

Page 49 The Interregnum

1. The King had been executed by Parliament [1]
2. Named after one of the leaders of Parliament, Praise-God Barebones [1]
3. A fine or prison [1]
4. His body was put on trial and hung at Tyburn, and his head was removed [1]

For questions 5 and 6 see Mark Scheme A.

5. Your answer should give an opinion and at least three examples. Examples may include:
   - Cromwell became Lord Protector. He retained the support of a strong army and was popular. He attempted to introduce a fair method of sharing power. He tried to ensure that the country was religious.
   - Royalists accused him of being responsible for the execution of the King. He imposed strict laws and rules on the country, which many people disliked. He had to use the army to run the country.
6. Your answer might include the following reasons, giving three different negative outcomes and backed up with facts.
   - Strict rules were introduced and many activities were banned for being immoral.

- Cromwell imposed military government on the people of England with the rule of the Major-Generals.
- Cromwell raised taxes and was seen as being greedy.
- He was accused of having the King executed for his own personal gain.

Pages 50–65 Revise Questions

Page 51 Quick Test: British Transatlantic Slave Trade 1
1. Timbuktu
2. 12 million
3. The Middle Passage
4. At auction
5. Whipped; forced to wear a punishment collar; sold away from your family; hung

Page 53 Quick Test: British Transatlantic Slave Trade 2
1. Olaudah Equiano
2. Thomas Clarkson
3. It banned the buying and selling of slaves
4. Abraham Lincoln
5. 1865

Page 55 Quick Test: Britain as the First Industrial Nation 1
1. Arkwright
2. 75 per cent
3. 500 000
4. 14 hours
5. Josiah Wedgwood

Page 57 Quick Test: Britain as the First Industrial Nation 2
1. Tuberculosis
2. Cholera
3. It was only a guideline, wasn't strictly enforced and was abolished 10 years later
4. Polluting rivers
5. Working hours

Page 59 Quick Test: Democratic Reform 1
1. Men over 21 with property
2. Bribery
3. An extension of the franchise and a fairer system by removing regional differences
4. 1.25 million
5. 500

Page 61 Quick Test: Democratic Reform 2
1. 1.9 million
2. It contained forged signatures
3. 2.5 million
4. Between 3 000 and 4 000
5. Living and working conditions got better

Page 63 Quick Test: Women's Suffrage 1
1. Adultery, cruelty or desertion
2. To allow them to keep income and property after marriage
3. Millicent Fawcett

4. Emmeline Pankhurst and her daughters Christabel and Sylvia
5. 'Deeds not words'

Page 65 Quick Test: Women's Suffrage 2
1. They were arrested after interrupting a political meeting
2. 250 000 to 500 000
3. Throw an axe into the Prime Minister's carriage and burn down the Theatre Royal
4. She was knocked down by the King's horse
5. 1928

> ## Pages 66–69 **Review Questions**

Page 66 The Peasants' Revolt
1. Between 50 000 and 60 000 [1]
2. Attacked the homes of the King's advisers [1]
3. The Bishop of London, the Royal Treasurer, and John Legge, organiser of the Poll Tax [1]
4. 1500 [1]

For questions 5 and 6 see Mark Scheme A.
5. A good answer would fully describe and explain the following:
   - The peasants were mainly from only Essex and Kent, not the whole country.
   - Their leader, Wat Tyler, was killed by the Mayor of London.
   - Richard II promised to give the peasants what they wanted.
   - The King used the army to crush the rebels.
   - Richard II reneged on his promises.
   - The peasants were poorly armed.
6. A good answer would fully describe and explain the following:
   - The Poll Tax was withdrawn.
   - Eventually villeinage came to an end and all Englishmen were freemen.
   - The King still ruled, without giving in to the peasants' demands.
   - Lords were forced to pay their peasants wages.

Page 67 Reformation and Counter Reformation
1. Nine years old [1]
2. Religious statues and paintings [1]
3. A rebellion against Henry in the north of England [1]
4. Appointment of the Archbishop of Canterbury and the bishops [1]

For questions 5 and 6 see Mark Scheme A.
5. A good answer would fully cover the following reasons:
   - Many monks were no longer performing their duties properly.
   - Henry VIII wanted to own monastic lands, to increase his wealth.
   - Henry and his advisers no longer believed monks played a useful part in religion.

- Henry wanted to increase his own power at the expense of the Church by taking more land.
6. A good answer would fully describe and explain the following differences:
   - Henry VIII had kept most Catholic religious services.
   - Edward VI changed how churches were organised: the altar was replaced by a table, church walls were whitewashed, statues and paintings were removed.
   - Edward VI introduced the Book of Common Prayer, containing new religious services.
   - Edward VI dissolved (closed) the last remaining monasteries, completing the work of Henry VIII.

Page 68 The English Civil War
1. Henrietta Maria [1]
2. William Laud [1]
3. 1500 [1]
4. John Bradshaw [1]
5. **One mark** for each valid observation (**5 marks** maximum). You might include the following observations:
   - It shows people fainting in shock.
   - It conveys that there was a large crowd/it was an important event.
   - You can see a boy trying to catch the King's blood.
   - A drawback is that it doesn't tell us what happened after the execution.
   - Another drawback is that it is mainly from the point of view of the crowd rather than Cromwell.

For question 6 see Mark Scheme A.
6. Your answer might include the following reasons, with the best answers looking at both sides of the argument.
   - Drew at Edgehill but won at Marston Moor before he was really important.
   - At Naseby his New Model Army crushed the King and gained a decisive victory.
   - Cromwell signed Charles's death warrant.

Page 69 The Interregnum
1. Execution of Charles I [1]
2. Its role was to implement domestic and foreign policy [1]
3. Meet every three years and stay in session for five months [1]
4. General Monck's army [1]

For question 5 see Mark Scheme A.
5. Your answer might include the following examples, backed up with facts:
   - England became a republic and Parliament ruled the country.
   - The Barebones Parliament contained 140 Puritans.
   - The Council of State contained army and civilian members.
   - The army was strong and remained loyal to Oliver Cromwell.

6. **One mark** for each valid observation (**5 marks** maximum). You might include the following observations:
   - It shows Cromwell accepting the role of Lord Protector.
   - Cromwell needed the support of the army.
   - Some MPs look angry because they are shaking their fists.
   - A drawback is that it doesn't explain why Cromwell is being offered the role of Lord Protector.

Pages 70–73 Practice Questions

Page 70 British Transatlantic Slave Trade

1. The Americas [1]
2. Young women [1]
3. 1807 [1]
4. 1861–65 [1]

For questions 5 and 6 see Mark Scheme A.

5. Your answer should give details about capture, the Middle Passage and auctions. Possible detail includes:
   - Chiefs/paid Africans were often used to capture slaves.
   - Conditions on the Middle Passage were horrific and sometimes two-thirds of slaves died onboard.
   - Many families were separated at slave auctions.
6. Your answer should give details about the role of at least three abolitionists and reach a judgement about which was the most important. Possible detail includes:
   - Olaudah Equiano had first-hand experience of being a slave.
   - Wilberforce raised the issue in Parliament 18 times.
   - Clarkson devoted 60 years of his life to ending slavery.

Page 71 Britain as the First Industrial Nation

1. Coal [1]
2. James Watt [1]
3. Cholera [1]
4. The Public Health Act [1]

For questions 5 and 6 see Mark Scheme A.

5. Your answer should detail at least three factors contributing to industrialisation. These could include:
   - Old methods of production were not meeting demand.
   - A rising population led to a rising demand for goods.
   - Improvements in science and technology.
6. Your answer should consider a variety of dangers. These could include:
   - Information about dangers in the factories, e.g. scalping, long working hours, punishments.
   - Details about workers' living conditions.
   - Information about epidemics and infectious disease, e.g. cholera and TB.

Page 72 Democratic Reform

1. 1832 [1]
2. An area that had a small number of voters who could be bribed easily [1]

3. 1.5 million people [1]
4. Secret Ballot Act [1]

For questions 5 and 6 see Mark Scheme A.

5. Your answer should explain at least three examples of unfairness. Examples may include:
   - The power and influence of local landowners.
   - Bribery and threats of violence, because voting was not secret.
   - Industrial towns and cities such as Manchester having no MPs.
   - Ordinary, working-class people not being represented in Parliament.
6. Your answer might include the following reasons, giving three different negative outcomes and backed up with facts and figures:
   - Parliament ignoring Chartist petitions, despite being signed by 1.25 million people.
   - Violent disturbances leading to arrest and imprisonment of Chartist leaders.
   - Forging signatures on petitions.
   - Lack of support for marches and the failure to win their six key demands.

Page 73 Women's Suffrage

1. It was assumed that husbands made all the important decisions [1]
2. Allowed women to keep income and property after marriage [1]
3. 1909 [1]
4. Women aged 30 or over who owned property [1]

For questions 5 and 6 see Mark Scheme A.

5. Your answer should give an opinion and at least three reasons. Examples of the importance of the Pankhursts are:
   - Women's Social and Political Union founded by Emmeline, Christabel and Sylvia in 1903.
   - Their motto was 'Deeds not words' and they believed in direct action.
   - Law breaking, violence and hunger strikes were all acceptable campaign methods.
   - They disrupted a meeting in Manchester in 1905 and demanded the right to vote.
6. Your answer might include the following reasons, giving three different negative outcomes and backed up with facts.
   - Women were often treated poorly, even if they were married.
   - Women could not become MPs or vote.
   - There was no particular political focus for the campaigns.
   - The Suffragists were only set up in 1897, and believed in peaceful tactics.

Page 75 Quick Test: The First World War 1

1. Archduke Franz Ferdinand
2. Because of the poor treatment of Serbians living in Bosnia
3. Dreadnought
4. Machine guns, tanks and poison gas
5. Heat and disease

Page 77 Quick Test: The First World War 2

1. General Pétain
2. General Haig
3. Pals Battalions, where groups of men from the same area fought together, were wiped out
4. £6.6 billion
5. War Guilt Clause

Page 79 Quick Test: The Second World War 1

1. It was done secretly; Britain and France were more concerned with the Soviet Union
2. He invaded the country and forced a fixed vote
3. He claimed people living there were German and wanted union with Germany
4. Hitler ignored it
5. The Nazi–Soviet Pact

Page 81 Quick Test: The Second World War 2

1. Lightning war (speedy)
2. From the beach by boat
3. Luftwaffe
4. 3 million
5. 200 000

Page 83 Quick Test: The Creation of the Welfare State 1

1. David Lloyd George
2. Seebohm Rowntree
3. 70
4. 1906
5. 1 million

Page 85 Quick Test: The Creation of the Welfare State 2

1. Beveridge
2. Want, Disease, Squalor, Ignorance, Idleness
3. Aneurin Bevan
4. 15
5. Prescription charges

Page 87 Quick Test: Britain's Place in the World 1945–Present 1

1. Electricity, gas, water and health
2. 58 million
3. By rebuilding it after the war
4. 12 million
5. Demand had declined because homes now used gas, oil or electricity

Page 89 Quick Test: Britain's Place in the World 1945–Present 2

1. Choose when to or whether to have children
2. They had more freedom from their parents' control

3. NATO in 1949, and the European Community in 1973
4. There were lots of public service strikes
5. 'Things can only get better'

Page 90 British Transatlantic Slave Trade

1. Ku Klux Klan [1]
2. Cotton [1]
3. The Committee for the Abolition of African Slavery [1]
4. Union Army [1]
5. **One mark** for each valid observation (**5 marks** maximum). You might include the following observations:
    *   Musical instruments – preserving cultural identity.
    *   Might show jumping the broom tradition.
    *   Slaves look well dressed – some slaves were well cared for.
    *   A drawback is that it is only an example of one plantation – it is painted by the owner so it might make it look better than it was.
    *   It also doesn't show slave punishments.

For question 6 see Mark Scheme A.

6. Your answer might include the following reasons, with the best answers looking at a wide range of points.
    *   Punishments such as beatings, lynchings and killings.
    *   Trauma such as being sold away from family; having name changed.

Page 91 Britain as the First Industrial Nation

1. Four [1]
2. Louis Pasteur [1]
3. Four years old [1]
4. Smallpox vaccination made compulsory [1]
5. **One mark** for each valid observation (**5 marks** maximum). You might include the following observations:
    *   A water pump could be a source of cholera.
    *   Cholera was a common cause of death, particularly in children.
    *   John Snow's work was recognised after he removed the pump on Broad Street.
    *   The poor were most at risk; you can see these children are poor by looking at their clothes.
    *   Little had changed by this point; many people were still reliant on dirty water despite Snow's work, as the source shows lots of children collecting water.

For question 6 see Mark Scheme A.

6. Your answer might include the following reasons, with the best answers focusing clearly on importance.
    *   Up to this point, incorrect theories such as 'miasma' had been used to explain disease.
    *   There had been many epidemics of infectious disease at this time; now it was possible to develop strategies to cure them.

- It allowed scientists such as Snow to explain their work and find greater acceptance of their findings.

Page 92 Democratic Reform
1. Manchester, Sheffield and Leeds [1]
2. 30 000 [1]
3. Benjamin Disraeli [1]
4. Take Saturday afternoon off [1]

For question 5 see Mark Scheme A.

5. Your answer should explain at least two important developments. Examples may include:
   - Two-thirds of men could now vote.
   - The number of voters tripled to 6 million.
   - Voters in different areas were given the same voting rights.
6. **One mark** for each valid observation (**5 marks** maximum.) You might include the following observations:
   - The uprising was popular because the crowd were cheering and enthusiastic.
   - The government thought the situation would become very violent so they brought in the army.
   - There was a high number of casualties.
   - A drawback is that it doesn't explain how the uprising ended, and is only one opinion of the event.

Page 93 Women's Suffrage
1. 1903 [1]
2. 30 [1]
3. Home Office, Treasury and *Daily Mail* offices [1]
4. To allow soldiers and sailors fighting in the war the right to vote [1]

For question 5 see Mark Scheme A.

5. Your answer should give an opinion and at least three reasons. Examples could include:
   - Sending Suffragettes to prison attracted lots of publicity.
   - Women in prison went on hunger strike.
   - Hunger strikers were later force fed by prison doctors.
   - When women were released from prison, they were weak and suffering ill health.
6. **One mark** for each valid observation (**5 marks** maximum). You might include the following observations:
   - They used violence to gain attention.
   - The government believed that the Suffragettes were a danger to society.
   - MPs failed to support the cause because of the increase in violence.
   - The government had promised to support the Suffragettes, but changed their mind in 1913.

Pages 94–97 Practice Questions

Page 94 The First World War
1. August 1914 [1]
2. Trench foot [1]
3. General Pétain [1]
4. Gallipoli [1]

For questions 5 and 6 see Mark Scheme A.

5. Your answer should give an opinion and compare it to two others. Possible causes are:
   - The assassination of Archduke Franz Ferdinand.
   - The arms race.
   - Empires.
   - The alliance system.
6. Your answer might include the following reasons, giving three different negative outcomes and backed up with facts and figures:
   - There were 20 000 dead and 20 000 injured on the first day alone.
   - General Haig was heavily criticised for not changing tactics.
   - In five months the British only advanced five miles.

Page 95 The Second World War
1. Hitler claimed German land should be protected by German troops [1]
2. With a policy called Appeasement [1]
3. The USSR and Germany agreed not to fight each other [1]
4. To fight Communism, and for *Lebensraum* [1]

For questions 5 and 6 see Mark Scheme A.

5. Your answer may include the following examples:
   - Initial persecution from 1933 tended to be non-violent.
   - Jewish people lost their businesses and had their freedom restricted.
   - During *Kristallnacht*, many Jewish homes, businesses and synagogues were destroyed, persecution now became openly violent.
   - Jewish people were rounded up and forced into ghettos, many died from disease or starvation.
   - The 'Final Solution' involved the use of gas chambers and death camps.
6. Your answer might include the following reasons, giving three different positive outcomes and backed up with facts.
   - Britain had developed radar technology to detect German aircraft.
   - Britain was not invaded by the German army.
   - It demonstrated the strength of the RAF.
   - Hitler called off Operation Sealion after only two months.

Page 96 The Creation of the Welfare State
1. The Labour Party [1]
2. The Boer War [1]
3. Operating theatres [1]
4. 1948 [1]

For questions 5 and 6 see Mark Scheme A.

5. Your answer should give an opinion and compare it to two others. Possible causes are:
   - The Labour Party was emerging as the 'voice of the working class' and talked of the need for reform.

- The Boer War highlighted the poor health of the working class.
- The work of social investigators showed the need for reform.
- The genuine charitable motivation of people such as Lloyd George.

6. Your answer might include the following reasons:
   - The Beveridge Report made recommendations based around the Five Giants of Evil.
   - The evacuation programme highlighted child poverty.
   - Medical facilities improved to cope with air raids.
   - There was a change in attitudes about political involvement in people's lives.

Page 97 Britain's Place in the World 1945–Present

1. 1954   [1]
2. Australia, New Zealand and South Africa   [1]
3. 1955   [1]
4. Introduction of a three-day working week and electricity rationing   [1]

For questions 5 and 6 see Mark Scheme A.

5. Your answer should give an opinion and compare it to two others. Examples of changes since 1945 may include:
   - Huge population increase from 47 million up to 58 million.
   - Changes in work with the disappearance of traditional industries such as coal mining, ship building and steel.
   - Social changes and increasing ownership of household goods and electrical items.
   - Political change, introduction of the NHS and the government trying to ensure equality for all.

6. Your answer might include the following reasons, giving three different positive outcomes and backed up with facts.
   - Introduction of the contraceptive pill and legalised abortion.
   - The growth of youth culture, including changes in pop music and youth consumerism.
   - Women's changing role in society, and an increase in the number of women in work.
   - Lowering of the voting age to 18.

Pages 98–105 **Revise Questions**

Page 99 Quick Test: Migration To and From the British Isles 1

1. To guard Hadrian's Wall
2. 14 000
3. NHS; London Transport
4. Sensationalist ones about unclean behaviour and criminal activity
5. Notting Hill

Page 101 Quick Test: Migration To and From the British Isles 2

1. Puritanism
2. Boston
3. Dysentery and smallpox

4. Potatoes
5. £200 in today's money

Page 103 Quick Test: USA in the 20th Century 1

1. Less than $300
2. Coal and rail
3. An illegal bar
4. 1920
5. 13 million

Page 105 Quick Test: USA in the 20th Century 2

1. Western Europe
2. Nuclear weapons
3. 125 000
4. Washington
5. 1965

Pages 106–109 **Review Questions**

Page 106 The First World War

1. Gavrilo Princip   [1]
2. 214 000   [1]
3. Enemy shelling   [1]
4. The War Guilt Clause   [1]
5. **One mark** for each valid observation (**5 marks** maximum). You might include the following observations:
   - Worries that people would starve.
   - Worries about widespread poverty.
   - Newspapers often show common opinion.
   - A drawback is that a cartoon might exaggerate.
   - It also mainly focuses on reparations, not other areas of the treaty.

For question 6 see Mark Scheme A.

6. Your answer might include mention of the following problems:
   - Unprepared for new technologies used by the enemy such as machine guns and mustard gas.
   - Rats; water causing disease/infections such as trench foot.

Page 107 The Second World War

1. 99 per cent   [1]
2. They did not want to risk the possibility of war   [1]
3. Operation Sealion   [1]
4. Over 6 million   [1]

For question 5 see Mark Scheme A.

5. Your answer should give an opinion and at least three different reasons. Examples may include:
   - Hitler's order for the invasion of the Soviet Union in 1941.
   - The D-Day landings, which took place in 1944.
   - The German army was attacked in both the West and East.
   - Millions of soldiers were killed during the war in the East.

6. **One mark** for each valid observation (**5 marks** maximum). You might include the following observations:
   - Britain had to prevent the invasion in order to end the war.
   - British people were encouraged to do their duty to help the country
   - Britain also relied on Commonwealth nations for support.
   - It shows the government understood how serious the Battle was.
   - A drawback is that it does not explain how Britain was to prepare for the invasion.

Page 108 The Creation of the Welfare State
1. Dirty water and cholera [1]
2. Germany [1]
3. 45 [1]
4. Doctors' throats [1]
5. **One mark** for each valid observation (**5 marks** maximum). You might include the following observations:
   - Doctors thought the government was interfering with their work.
   - They were opposed on political grounds.
   - Many doctors were conservative; Bevan was a Labour MP.
   - The source doesn't tell us about disagreements over pay.
   - It doesn't tell us how the issue was resolved.

For question 6 see Mark Scheme A.
6. Your answer might include the following reasons, with the best answers looking at a wide range of points:
   - Pensions not issued until 70 when life expectancy was 45 for most.
   - Labour Exchanges often provided only low-paid, part-time jobs.
   - Health care from National Insurance didn't extend to a worker's family.

Page 109 Britain's Place in the World 1945–Present
1. 1956 [1]
2. USA and USSR [1]
3. The Beatles and the Rolling Stones [1]
4. 82 per cent [1]

For questions 5 and 6 see Mark Scheme A.
5. Your answer should describe at least two different changes. Examples of changes since 1945 may include:
   - The number of women in work doubled from 6 million to 12 million.
   - The disappearance of traditional industries such as coal mining, ship building and steel.
   - Huge growth in the use of technology.
   - The number of self-employed workers increased.
6. Your answer might include the following reasons, backed up with facts:
   - The introduction of the NHS and advanced medical care.

- Increase in immigration from the Commonwealth following the Second World War.
- Increase in life expectancy, with 16 per cent of the population over 65.

Pages 110–111 **Practice Questions**

Page 110 Migration To and From the British Isles
1. 800 million [1]
2. The Caribbean [1]
3. Smallpox [1]
4. Their Catholic beliefs [1]

For questions 5 and 6 see Mark Scheme A.
5. Your answer should explain the impact of:
   - The shortage of workers.
   - Recruitment campaigns for companies such as London Transport and the NHS.
   - The impact of Acts such as the British Nationality Act 1948.
6. Your answer might include the following problems:
   - The Notting Hill riots.
   - Cultural and language barriers.
   - Discrimination.

Page 111 USA in the 20th Century
1. Fridges, radios, washing machines, vacuum cleaners [1]
2. Led to violence and immoral behaviour [1]
3. Suspicious of each other, but no actual fighting [1]
4. End segregation in all public places [1]

For questions 5 and 6 see Mark Scheme A.
5. Your answer should give an opinion and compare it to two others. Examples of prosperity or poverty are:
   - Rising standards of living and income.
   - Stock market boom and huge investment in shares.
   - Boom in motor industry and production of cars.
   - Wealth was not evenly distributed; many poorly paid jobs.
   - Decline of old industries, and growth of urban poverty.
6. Your answer might include the following reasons, giving three different negative outcomes and backed up with facts and figures:
   - Desire to prevent Communism in the Far East.
   - Huge increases in numbers of US soldiers sent to fight.
   - Difficult fighting conditions in the Vietnamese jungle.
   - Failure of peace talks in 1968 meant the war continued until 1973.

Pages 112–113 **Review Questions**

Page 112 Migration To and From the British Isles
1. 12th century [1]
2. Slaves [1]

3. The successful harvest of 1621   [1]
4. Taking their women   [1]
5. **One mark** for each valid point (**5 marks** maximum). You might include the following points:
   - It is useful in telling us there was a lot of racism towards immigrants.
   - It doesn't tell us about poor housing conditions.
   - It doesn't tell us about race riots.
   - It doesn't tell us about young white men attacking immigrants over women.
   - It doesn't tell us about language/cultural barriers.

For question 6 see Mark Scheme A.

6. Your answer should include a description of some of the following:
   - Jewish moneylenders recorded in the 12th century.
   - Romans bringing Africans to guard Hadrian's Wall.
   - Some seamen from the Empire settled in Britain after the First World War.

Page 113 USA in the 20th Century

1. 1924   [1]
2. 4 million   [1]
3. 5000   [1]
4. 1865   [1]

For question 5 see Mark Scheme A.

5. Your answer should give an opinion and explain at least three reasons. Examples may include:
   - Prohibition meant that producing alcohol became a criminal offence.
   - Criminal gangs took advantage and fought for control of specific areas.
   - There was bribery and corruption among the police and judges.

6. **One mark** for each valid observation (**5 marks** maximum). You might include the following observations:
   - It shows the Soviet Union and the USA in a stalemate.
   - Both leaders are sitting on nuclear weapons, to indicate how serious the situation is.
   - The Soviet leader is sweating, which demonstrates a tense situation.
   - A drawback is that the origin of the cartoon is unknown, this might affect its reliability.
   - Another drawback is that it is only one point of view and does not give the whole story.

Pages 114–125 **Mixed Test-Style Questions**

Page 114

1. **One mark** for each valid observation (**5 marks** maximum). You might include the following observations:
   - It shows soldiers fighting in battle.
   - One soldier has an arrow in his eye – this could be Harold.
   - It shows what soldiers wore and the weapons they used.

- It only shows one aspect of battle.
- It was produced over 10 years after the event so it may not be very accurate.

2. **One mark** for each valid observation (**5 marks** maximum). You might include the following observations:
   - It is one person's view.
   - It is written over 10 years after the Black Death.
   - It doesn't mention the belief that bad air was a cause.
   - It doesn't mention the belief that the Black Death was a punishment from God.

Page 116

1. **One mark** for each correct answer (**5 marks** maximum).
   a) False b) True c) True d) False e) True

2. **One mark** for each valid observation (**5 marks** maximum). You might include the following observations:
   - It shows that Emmeline Pankhurst tried to justify her violent actions.
   - It shows that the Pankhursts wanted publicity for their cause, particularly from the newspapers.
   - It shows that Emmeline Pankhurst was an educated woman because she wrote a book.
   - It doesn't tell us about the effect or importance of non-violent protest organised by Millicent Fawcett.
   - It is only Emmeline Pankhurst's opinion. It does not look at events in detail.

Page 118

1. **One mark** for each valid observation (**5 marks** maximum). You might include the following observations:
   - It shows children under machines.
   - It shows inadequate clothing.
   - There is poor ventilation – there are very few windows.
   - There are no safety guards.
   - There are no supervisors.

2. **One mark** for each valid observation (**5 marks** maximum). You might include the following observations:
   - It is one person's view.
   - It is written only half way through the war.
   - It does not mention common views of life in the trenches.
   - The writer might have lied to reassure his family.
   - He seems very literate and possibly not working class so may not be representative.

Page 120

For marks for these questions see Mark Scheme A.

1. You need to use your imagination to answer this question, describing your motives and feelings with as much detail as possible. Your motives will depend on what kind of person you imagine yourself being:
   - If a king, going on a Crusade would bring you extra power and wealth and the support of the Pope.

- If a lord, you would be going on a Crusade to gain wealth and land.
- If a knight, you might be going on a Crusade because your king and lord demanded it. Also, as a knight you had a duty to protect the Christian Church.
- Ordinary people went on Crusades to gain extra credit to get into heaven.
- Criminals and thieves went on Crusades because it would mean their punishments would come to an end.
- Priests and monks went on Crusades to participate in a holy war to regain the Holy Land.

2. Your answer should give a full explanation of the factors that forced King John to sign Magna Carta, and should be supported with evidence. The main factors, in brief, were as follows:
   - King John faced major financial problems.
   - He also had major problems with the Church.
   - King John had lost lots of English land in France.
   - John had a quarrel with the barons, which he was losing.
   - John was forced to sign to end this quarrel and to help end his other problems.

3. A good answer would cover the following points, and each point would be supported by a full explanation and evidence:
   - The Reformation changed England from a Catholic country to a Protestant country.
   - The King, rather than the Pope, was Head of the Church.
   - Religious services were conducted in English instead of Latin.
   - The King gained immense wealth and power from the Church.
   - The monasteries were dissolved.

Page 122

For marks for these questions see Mark Scheme A.

1. A good answer would cover the following points, supported by evidence:
   - It was a conflict between two groups in the same country.
   - It involved the trial and execution of a monarch.
   - It was followed by a period without a monarchy.

2. A good answer would cover the following points, supported by evidence:
   - From 1649, stability of government was required following the execution of the King. Cromwell retained the loyalty and support of the army.
   - Cromwell had been a key figure in the execution of Charles and the destruction of the monarchy.
   - The Lord Protector had many of the powers of a king, but was not answerable to Parliament.

- Cromwell feared many people would argue that he had helped execute the King for his own personal benefit.

3. A good answer would cover the following points, supported by evidence:
   - Poverty among Irish farmers intensified by mass starvation following the disastrous potato harvest of 1845.
   - Millions faced a difficult and cramped journey to the USA, often only affordable for one family member.
   - On arrival in New York, immigrants had to undergo stringent medical checks at Ellis Island.
   - Those able to stay faced life in a squalid tenement block and being stigmatised for their Catholic beliefs.

Page 124

For marks for these questions see Mark Scheme A.

1. A good answer would cover the following points, supported by evidence:
   - Support due to a number of political, economic and social motivations.
   - The manifesto of the emerging Labour Party focused heavily on welfare reform. A growing trade union movement was also pressing for better working conditions.
   - Recruitment of soldiers for the Boer War had shown most working-class men to be unfit for service.
   - Lloyd George had genuine compassion for the working class.

2. A good answer would cover the following points, supported by evidence:
   - The Soviet army appeared to be very weak and could easily be defeated in 1941.
   - Three million soldiers were sent to fight and the Germans planned to use the tactic of Blitzkrieg warfare.
   - Early German successes meant that Moscow and Leningrad were easily captured.
   - The Battle of Stalingrad was brutal, and the harsh conditions meant that many soldiers starved or froze to death.

3. A good answer would cover the following points, supported by evidence:
   - The development of popular culture – including music, film and fashion.
   - The impact of the legalisation of abortion and the introduction of the contraceptive pill.
   - Increasing ownership of consumer goods.
   - The rise of the teenager, youth consumerism and the changing roles of women.

Timeline

1066 Battle of Hastings; William is crowned king.

1066–76 Rebellion of Hereward the Wake.

1069 Rebellion against William in northern England.

1085–86 Domesday Book compiled.

1087 William I dies.

1096–99 The First Crusade.

1147–49 The Second Crusade.

1170 Archbishop Thomas A'Becket murdered in Canterbury.

1187 Battle of Hattin.

1189–92 The Third Crusade.

1199 John becomes King.

1202–04 The Fourth Crusade.

1204 John loses Normandy to France.

1205 John has a major argument with the Pope.

1209 The Pope excommunicates John.

1212 The Children's Crusade.

1214 War breaks out between John and the barons.

1215 John signs Magna Carta.

1265 England's first parliament meets.

June 1348 Black Death arrives in England at Melcombe Regis (Weymouth) in Dorset.

Aug 1348 Black Death hits Bristol.

Sept 1348 Black Death reaches London.

Jan 1349 Parliament stops meeting on account of the plague.

Jan–Feb 1349 Black Death spreads into East Anglia and the Midlands.

April 1349 Black Death reported in Wales.

July 1349 Black Death hits Ireland.

1377 Richard II becomes king at the age of 10.

1380 Poll Tax is introduced.

May–June 1381 Peasants' Revolt breaks out in Essex and Kent.

1381 Poll Tax is withdrawn.

1441 Portuguese capture a small group of Africans.

1500–1600 Europeans develop colonies in the Americas.

1500 The feudal system ends; all Englishmen are freemen.

1509 Henry VIII becomes King.

1533 Henry divorces Catherine of Aragon.

1534 Henry VIII makes himself Supreme Head of the Church in England.

1536 Henry begins closing monasteries.

1547 Edward VI makes England a Protestant country.

1553 Mary I becomes queen and the Counter Reformation begins.

1558 Mary I dies and is replaced by the Protestant Elizabeth I.

1619 First group of slaves arrive in North America.

1620 Pilgrim Fathers arrive in America.

August 1642 English Civil War breaks out.

October 1642 Battle of Edgehill.

July 1644 Battle of Marston Moor.

June 1645 Battle of Naseby.

January 1647 Charles is given to Parliament.

November 1647 Charles escapes.

August 1648 Charles is recaptured.

January 1649 Charles is executed; the monarchy is abolished and England becomes a republic.

1653 Cromwell and his army march to Parliament and close it down.

1653 Cromwell is elected as Lord Protector.

1655 Cromwell divides the country into districts and puts army Major-Generals in charge.

1655–57 The rule of the Major-Generals is established to stop opposition towards Cromwell and protect law and order.

1657 Cromwell is offered the crown, but refuses. He is given extra powers as Lord Protector.

1658 Cromwell dies of ill health.

1658 Cromwell's son Richard becomes Lord Protector.

1659 Richard resigns as Lord Protector due to lack of support.

1660 Charles II returns from Holland and restores the monarchy.

1700s Northern US states abolish slavery but it remains important in the South.

1769 Richard Arkwright invents water frame.

1769 James Watt improves steam engine.

1773 Scots arrive in Canada.

1807 The Slave Trade Abolition Act in Britain.

1820s Only men aged over 21 with property can vote.

1830 First passenger railway opens.

1832 Reform Act.

1833 The Slavery Abolition Act in Britain.

1836 London artisans form the London Working Men's Association.

1836 Chartist petition.

1839 Newport Uprising.

1840s Many Irish leave for America.

1848 Public Health Act.

1848 End of Chartism.

1853 Smallpox vaccination compulsory.

1854 Improvements in hospital hygiene.

1861–65 American Civil War.

1864 Factory Act – to improve standards and safety measures.

1865 Slavery is abolished in the Americas.

1867 Reform Act increases the number of men who can vote.

1870 Law passed to allow women to keep income and property after marriage.

1872 National Movement for Women's Suffrage formed.

1872 Secret Ballot Act attempts to end bribery and corruption.

1874 Factory Act reduces working hours.

1875 Public Health Act provides clean water in towns.

1894 Manchester ship canal opens.

1897 Millicent Fawcett forms the National Union of Women's Suffrage Societies.

1903 Women's Social and Political Union formed by the Pankhursts.

1905 Two members of the Suffragette movement arrested in Manchester.

1906 Suffragette protest at Downing Street.

1906 Free school meals.

1907 School Medical Inspectors Act.

1908 Children's Charter and old age pensions.

1908 Protest rally in Hyde Park.

1909 Labour Exchanges set up.

1911 National Insurance Act.

1911 220 women arrested for a series of violent protests.

1913 Emily Davison killed by a horse at the Epsom Derby.

June 1914 Franz Ferdinand assassinated.

August 1914 War breaks out.

February 1915 Gallipoli campaign begins.

December 1915 Gallipoli campaign ends in disaster.

1916 Lloyd George becomes Prime Minister.

Feb–July 1916 The Battle of Verdun.

July–Nov 1916 The Battle of the Somme.

11 November 1918 The First World War ends.

1918 Women over 30 who own property given the right to vote.

28 June 1919 The Treaty of Versailles signed.

1920 Prohibition introduced.

1928 All women given the right to vote in Britain.

1929 The Wall Street Crash, USA.

1929 St Valentine's Day Massacre, USA.

1931 Al Capone arrested.

1933 Prohibition ended.

1933 Germany begins to rearm.

1936 German troops march into the Rhineland.

1938 Austria and Germany unite.

1938 Appeasement agreement (Munich Pact).

1939 Hitler invades Czechoslovakia and Poland.

1939 Britain and France declare war on Germany.

1940 Evacuation of Dunkirk.

1940 The Battle of Britain.

1941 Germany invades the Soviet Union.

1942 Soviet Union starts to push the German army back.

1943 German army surrender at Stalingrad.

1944 D-Day landings take place.

1944 Education Act (implemented 1945); school leaving age raised to 15.

1945 Germany surrenders; end of Second World War.

1945 Labour responsible for post-war consensus.

1945 Family allowances introduced.

1946 National Insurance Act extended.

1948 National Assistance Act to help those not covered by National Insurance.

1948 British Nationality Act.

1948 National Health Service introduced.

1949 Britain joins NATO.

1955 Rosa Parks and the bus boycott.

1955 Commercial television begins.

1962 Commonwealth Immigration Act in Britain.

1963 Martin Luther King delivers his 'I have a dream' speech.

1964 Civil Rights Act passed in USA.

1965 and 1968 Race Relations Act in Britain.

1968 Commonwealth Immigrants Act in Britain.

1968 500 000 soldiers fighting in Vietnam.

1971 Immigration Act in Britain.

1972 Miners go on strike.

1973 Britain joins the European Community.

1979 The Winter of Discontent leads to Labour losing the general election.

1979 Margaret Thatcher becomes Britain's first female prime minister.

1991 The Internet becomes available to the public.

1997 Labour, led by Tony Blair, wins the general election.

Index

Acknowledgements

Cover & p1 © David Maska. Shutterstock.com, © Morphart Creation/shutterstock.com and © Nataliavand/Shutterstock.com; P7 © UPPA/Photoshot; P21 © Illustrated London News Ltd/Mary Evans; P37 © Mary Evans Picture Library; P50 © Classic Image/Alamy; P58 © liszt collection/Alamy; P58 © Classic Image/Alamy; P59 © Mary Evans Picture Library/Alamy; P68 © The Art Gallery Collection/Alamy; P69 © Look and Learn; P90 © Image Asset Management Ltd/Alamy; P91 © Mary Evans Picture Library; P92 Extract from Aspects of History – Britain 1750-1900: Industry, Trade & Politics by Chris Andrews (Nelson Thornes, 2002) by S Pickering (OUP, 1965), reprinted by permission of the publishers, Oxford Universlty Press; P106 © Thomas Theodor Heine/DACS; P107 Extract from Winston Churchill's Their Finest Hour speech in June 1940; P112 © Neil Kenlock; P113 © Associated Newspapers Ltd/Solo Syndication; P114 © Ancient Art & Architecture Collection Ltd/Alamy; P118 © Science Museum/Science & Society Picture Library; All other images © Shutterstock.com

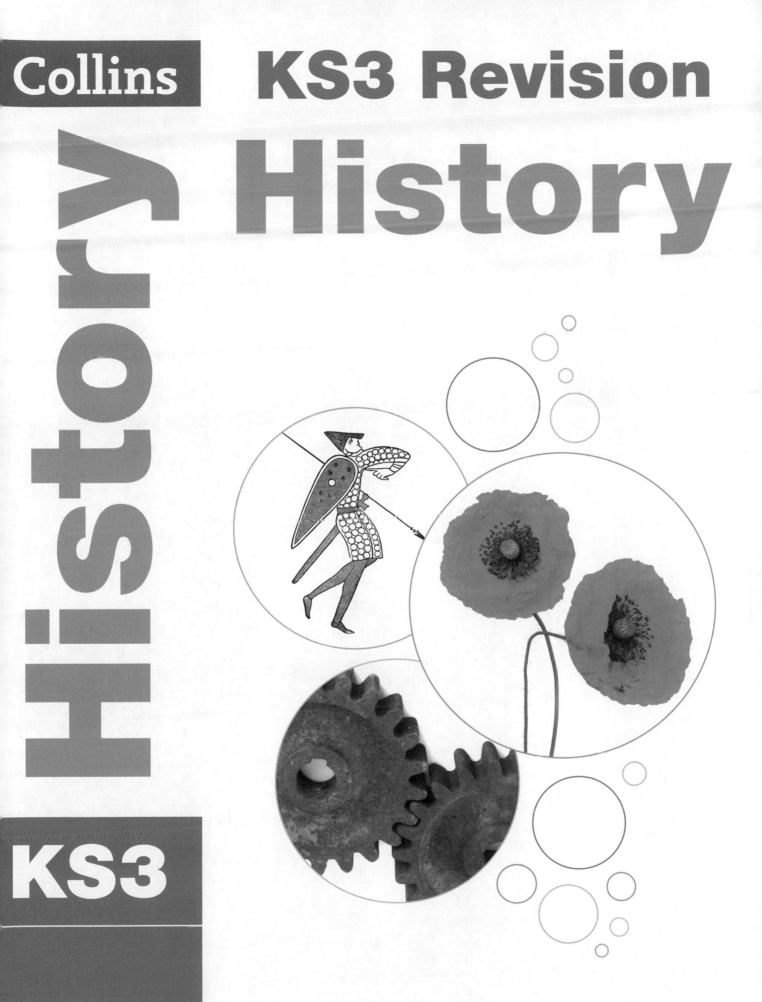

Collins

KS3 Revision
History

History

KS3

Workbook

**Philippa Birch, Steve McDonald
and Rachelle Pennock**

KS3 History Workbook

Contents

The Norman Conquest

1 Study Source A and then answer the questions that follow.

Source A: Part of the Bayeux Tapestry, which was created just after the Norman Conquest.

a) How many people can you see in total in Source A? _____ [1]

b) What weapons can you see in Source A?

_____

_____

_____ [4]

c) Look at the origin of the source (where the source comes from). Why do you think the source is reliable for explaining what happened during the Battle of Hastings? Explain your answer.

_____

_____

_____

_____ [2]

2 Study Sources A and B and then answer the questions that follow.

Source A: An illustration of a motte and bailey castle.

Source B: A modern historian's view.

Motte and bailey castles were not a good form of defence. They were weak as they were made out of wood rather than stone. This meant they could catch fire very easily. The keep (castle) was also quite small, meaning very few people could gather inside.

a) Look at Source A. Identify five forms of defence that a motte and bailey castle used.

_____

_____

_____ **[5]**

b) List three ways in which the motte and bailey castle's defences could be improved.

_____

_____ **[3]**

c) According to Source B, 'Motte and bailey castles were not a good form of defence'. Give one reason in favour of this statement and one against.

In favour: _____

_____

Against: _____

_____ **[4]**

Total Marks _____ / 18

Christendom and the Crusades

1 Explain what medieval people believed about going to heaven or hell. Give two examples for each answer.

Heaven: ....

....

....

....

Hell: ....

....

....

....

[4]

2 Why did all medieval churches have Doom paintings?

....

....

....

[2]

3 What other functions did medieval churches perform that churches still perform today?

....

....

....

....

[3]

4 Study Sources A and B and then answer the questions that follow.

Source A: A German monk describes the actions of some Crusaders as they passed through Germany on their way to Jerusalem.

> They suddenly attacked the Jews. They decapitated many and inflicted serious wounds, they destroyed their homes and synagogues, and divided a very great sum of looted money among themselves.

Source B: An extract from Pope Urban's speech of 1095.

You must run as quickly as you can to help your brothers living on the eastern shores. The Turks have overrun them, slaughtering and capturing many and destroying churches. They cut open their stomachs and tear out their most vital organs. They tie them to a stake, or drag them around and flog them. Jerusalem is the most important place in the world. All men going there who die, whether on the journey or while fighting the non-Christians, will immediately be forgiven their sins.

a) What is the aim of Source B? Give an example from the source to support your answer.

_____

_____

_____

_____ **[2]**

b) Compare Sources A and B. How are they different? Give one example to support your answer.

_____

_____

_____

_____ **[2]**

c) Look at the origin of the sources (where the sources come from). Why do you think they differ so much? Explain your answer.

_____

_____

_____

_____

_____

_____ **[4]**

Total Marks _____ / 17

Britain 1066–1509

Magna Carta

1. Study Sources A and B and then answer the questions that follow.

Source A: Extracts from Magna Carta.

- I will not make citizens pay taxes without asking the permission of the Lords.
- All free men will be given a fair trial before being put in prison.
- As the King, I will not interfere with the Church.
- Barons will only be fined if other barons believe they are guilty.
- Judges will not be bribed with money.

Source B: A modern historian's view.

The Magna Carta did not create a fair society for everybody in England. Only freemen were given fair trials, there was still a lot of bribery in some law courts and the Church still had lots of problems.

a) Use Source A to identify two groups of people who would have benefitted from King John signing Magna Carta.

_____

_____ [2]

b) Use Sources A and B to identify two groups of people who might not have benefitted from King John signing Magna Carta.

_____

_____ [2]

c) List two ways in which Magna Carta could have been made fairer.

_____

_____

_____ [2]

2 Study Sources A and B and then answer the questions that follow.

Source A: A modern historian's view.

> John was the worst King England has ever had. He lost lots of land such as Normandy, he was a terrible soldier and did not follow the teachings of Christianity.

Source B: A modern historian's view.

> King John was not a bad king, he was just unlucky. He was kind, intelligent and ensured that England became a safe country. By the time King John died, England was a much safer country than it had been previously.

a) Use Source A to explain why King John is seen to have been a bad king.
   Give two reasons.

   _____

   _____

   _____ **[2]**

b) Use Source B to explain why King John is seen to have been a good king.
   Give two reasons.

   _____

   _____

   _____ **[2]**

c) Compare Sources A and B. Can both interpretations of King John be correct?
   Explain your answer.

   _____

   _____

   _____ **[2]**

Total Marks _____ / 12

Britain 1066–1509

The Black Death

1 What did medieval people believe caused the Black Death? Give two examples.

....

....

.... **[2]**

2 Why do you think there were so many different ideas about what caused the Black Death? Give two reasons and explain your answers.

....

....

....

....

....

.... **[4]**

3 What does the Black Death teach us about attitudes towards Jews in medieval times? Give two answers.

....

....

.... **[2]**

4 Study Sources A and B and then answer the questions that follow.

Source A: Information collected from a modern historian about the impact of the Black Death.

- Food shortages
- Few people in towns and villages
- Increased dislike of Jews
- Unused farming land
- Increase in food prices

Source B: Workers carrying coffins and burying dead bodies, drawn during the Medieval period.

a) Using Source A, categorise the effects of the Black Death into social (effects on relationships between people) and economic (effects on money and business) factors.

Social: ....

....

Economic: ....

....
    [5]

b) Which source is the most useful to explain the impact of the Black Death? Give a reason to explain your choice.

....

....
    [2]

c) Which source is the most reliable for explaining the impact of the Black Death? Give a reason to explain your choice.

....

....
    [2]

Total Marks .... / 17

The Peasants' Revolt

1 Study Sources A and B and then answer the questions that follow.

Source A: A speech by the peasants' leader, John Ball.

> The rich have wines, spices, and fine bread, while we have only rye and water. It is by our labour that they can live so well. We are called slaves and if we do not perform our services we are beaten. Let us go to the King, he is young, and from him we may receive a favourable answer.

Source B: A government rule of law in the 1350s.

> If any workman in a man's service leaves the service without permission, he shall be imprisoned.

a) Is Source A in favour of or against the Peasants' Revolt? Give a reason for your answer.

....

....

.... **[2]**

b) Look at the origin of both sources (where the sources come from). Why do you think each source has a different opinion of the Peasants' Revolt? Mention both sources in your answer.

....

....

....

.... **[4]**

c) 'Because both sources state different views about the Peasants' Revolt, they cannot both be valid.' Do you agree with this statement? Give a reason for your opinion.

....

....

....

.... **[2]**

2 Study Sources A and B and then answer the questions that follow.

Source A: A picture of Wat Tyler speaking to peasants during the Peasants' Revolt.

Source B: A picture of Wat Tyler being killed with a sword by the Lord Mayor (bottom left of picture); the peasants are shown on the right.

a) How does Source A show that Wat Tyler was a good leader?

....

.... [2]

b) Compare Sources A and B. What differences can you see between how the peasants are portrayed? Give two examples.

....

.... [2]

c) Which source (A or B) shows Wat Tyler to be the better leader? Compare the sources and give a reason for your answer.

....

.... [2]

Total Marks .... / 14

Britain 1509–1745

Reformation and Counter-Reformation

1 Study Sources A and B and then answer the questions that follow.

Source A: A range of reasons for the Reformation, summarised by a modern historian.

- The Pope and priests cannot decide if you are to go to heaven – only God can do this.
- You cannot seek forgiveness from your sins by paying money to the Church.
- Priests should not teach people that they can buy help to enter heaven.
- It is better to give to the poor than to try to pay for your forgiveness.
- We should have the Bible in languages other than Latin.

Source B: A range of changes in the Catholic Church during the Counter-Reformation, summarised by a modern historian.

- More help was given to the poor and sick who were in need.
- There was active promotion of how priests could live a good life.
- An improvement in education and teaching for poor children.

a) Which two reasons for the Reformation do not focus on money?

....

.... **[2]**

b) Compare Sources A and B. Which reason for the Reformation has been acknowledged by the Catholic Church in Source B?

.... **[1]**

c) Which change in Source B do you think a supporter of the Reformation would be most happy with? Explain your answer.

....

....

....

.... **[2]**

2 Study Sources A and B and then answer the questions that follow.

Source A: The inside of a Catholic church.

Source B: The inside of a Protestant church.

a) What differences are there between the Catholic church in Source A and the Protestant church in Source B? Give two examples.

_____

_____ **[2]**

b) What similarities are there between the Catholic church in Source A and the Protestant church in Source B? Give three examples.

_____

_____ **[3]**

c) Using the sources and your own knowledge, what consequence would there be for religion in England from a growing number of Protestant churches? Explain your answer.

_____

_____ **[2]**

Total Marks _____ / 12

The English Civil War

1 Study Source A and then answer the question that follows.

Source A: A modern historian's view.

> Alongside his poor financial management and constant disregard for Parliament, Charles faced many issues regarding religion. His Catholic wife was deeply unpopular, as were the changes he made to church services. The burning of incense and gold decorations were seen as Catholic practices in Protestant England. His introduction of a new prayer book incensed [angered] the Scots.

Use Source A to identify two reasons for the Civil War. Explain your answer.

_____

_____

_____

_____ **[4]**

2 Name two key battles in the Civil War.

_____

_____ **[2]**

3 Why did the Parliamentarians win the Civil War?

_____

_____

_____

_____ **[3]**

4 Study Sources A and B and then answer the questions that follow.

Source A: A modern historian's view.

> It was very difficult to find anyone willing to execute the King. It is widely reported that the execution drew large crowds. Many were said to have fainted or gasped loudly once the execution was complete. It has been said that there was a feeling of great uncertainty following the execution as never before had a monarch been killed in this way, and England was left without a ruler.

Source B: A painting from approximately 1649 by an unknown artist.

a) Use Source B to describe the scene at Charles I's execution.

....

....

....

....

.... [5]

b) What can you learn from Source A about the atmosphere at the execution?

....

....

.... [3]

c) What are the two main reasons given in Source A for the uncertainty around Charles's death?

....

....

.... [2]

Total Marks .... / 19

Britain 1509–1745

1   Study Sources A and B and then answer the questions that follow.

Source A: From Nathanial Crouch, *A History of Oliver Cromwell*, 1692. Oliver Cromwell was known as Lord Protector during his time ruling England.

> Many people in our times… have great respect for the memory of Oliver Cromwell, as being a great man of devout religion and a great champion for the liberties [freedoms] of the nation.

Source B: Amended extract from John Evelyn's diary, 22 November 1658.

> I saw the superb funeral of the Protector today… and it was the most joyful funeral that I ever saw, there was not a single person who cried, the soldiers and the crowd celebrated with loud noise; drinking and taking tobacco in the streets as they went.

a) Give two examples that show the author of Source A supported Oliver Cromwell.

....

.... **[2]**

b) Describe Cromwell's funeral using evidence from Source B.

....

....

....

.... **[3]**

c) Explain which source (A or B) would be most useful to a historian trying to find out about Cromwell's rule.

....

....

....

....

....

.... **[5]**

2 Study Sources A and B and then answer the questions that follow.

Source A: A portrait of Charles II. Charles wears the Stuart Imperial State Crown.

Source B: A modern historian's view.

> Charles II was a popular king and was nicknamed the Merry Monarch. He loved the ceremony and dignity that came with being King, and enjoyed drinking, dancing and horse racing. Many people had disliked the harsh Puritan rule and laws under Cromwell, and Charles II restored many people's faith in the monarchy.

a) Using Source A, give five examples that show Charles II was a powerful king.

_____

_____

_____

_____ **[5]**

b) Use Sources A and B to describe in your own words why Charles II was a popular king.

_____

_____

_____

_____ **[5]**

Total Marks _____ / 20

British Transatlantic Slave Trade

1 Explain how the Triangular Trade worked.

....

....

....

....

....

....

....

....

....

.... **[6]**

2 Using your own knowledge, explain what life was like for slaves during the Middle Passage.

....

....

....

....

....

.... **[4]**

3 Study Sources A and B and then answer the questions that follow.

Source A: A modern historian's view.

Life on the plantations could be very hard. Punishments were brutal. In particular young men on large plantations faced gruelling jobs in the fields. However life was not the same for all slaves. Slaves on some plantations were treated relatively well by their owners. House slaves, who worked indoors, often faced more favourable conditions.

Source B: A poster produced in the Southern States of America to show what life was like for slaves on the plantations.

a) Use Source B to make four observations about what life was like for slaves.

....

....

....

.... **[4]**

b) Which source (A or B) is most reliable in showing what life was like for slaves on plantations, and why?

....

....

....

....

.... **[6]**

Total Marks .... / 20

Britain 1745–1901

Britain as the First Industrial Nation

1 Explain the change from the Domestic System to the Factory System.

....

....

....

....

....

....

[4]

2 Explain some of the problems workers faced in the new factories. Give three examples.

....

....

....

....

....

....

....

....

[6]

3 Name two things Josiah Wedgewood did to improve the lives of his workers.

....

....

....

[2]

4 Study Sources A and B and then answer the questions that follow.

Source A: A modern historian's view.

> Stockport thrived during the Industrial Revolution because of its proximity [closeness] to Manchester and the Peak District, maximising the potential for water power. It had a booming hat industry. However there were downsides too. The hat industry meant that many workers suffered the effects of mercury poisoning. The viaduct, which took 21 months to build, was the largest in the world when it opened, but many people had lost their lives during its construction. As with most towns, Stockport also saw the effects of pollution and poor living conditions during the industrial era.

Source B: A modern photo of Stockport Railway Viaduct.

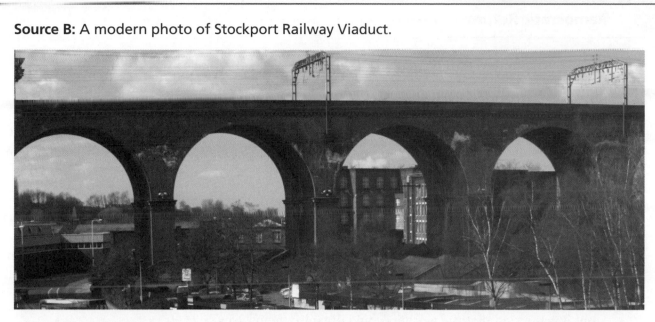

a) Which of the following can we learn from Source A about Stockport in the industrial era? Circle your answer(s).

i) A viaduct was built.

ii) There was a large hat industry.

iii) It had the first factory to use electricity. [2]

b) Having looked at both sources, explain the strengths and limitations of Source B for someone interested in the Stockport Viaduct.

_____

_____

_____

_____ [4]

c) Use the facts in Source A to explain one negative and one positive impact of the industrial era on Stockport.

Negative: _____

_____

Positive: _____

_____ [4]

Total Marks _____ / 22

Britain 1745–1901

Democratic Reform

1 Study Sources A and B and then answer the questions that follow.

Source A: Chartist leader Joseph Stevens in 1838.

> If any man is asked why he wanted the vote he would answer so that he could shelter himself and his family, have a good dinner on the table and have as much wages as would keep him in plenty.

Source B: A modern historian's view.

> The working class was not represented by the Great Reform Act of 1832, but a group called the Chartists developed in the late 1830s and [they] pressed for sweeping changes to the political system so that the working class was represented. Chartism came to an end in 1848 but it was a sign that the workers could organise themselves.

a) Which of the following can we learn from Source B?

   i) The Great Reform Act was passed in 1832.

   ii) Chartism ended in 1860.

   iii) Political change was needed. [2]

b) Use Source A to describe three reasons why this Chartist leader wanted the vote.

   ....

   ....

   .... [3]

c) Which source (A or B) is most reliable for a historian studying the Chartist movement and why?

   ....

   ....

   ....

   ....

   .... [5]

2 Study Source A and then answer the questions that follow.

Source A: A political cartoon from 1832 entitled 'The Reformers' Attack on the Old Rotten Tree'.

a) A rotten borough was an area that had a small number of voters who could be easily bribed. In this cartoon they are shown as birds in the tree. How many rotten boroughs are there in this source?

.... [1]

b) Are the reformers on the left or the right of this source?

.... [1]

c) This is a primary source. Why would this be useful to a historian?

....

....

.... [3]

d) What message is the artist trying to give about the need to reform the voting system?

....

....

....

.... [5]

Total Marks .... / 20

Women's Suffrage

1 Study Source A and then answer the questions that follow.

Source A: A political poster showing the treatment of suffragettes in prison. The graffiti on the prison wall reads 'Votes for Women'.

a) Which of the following can we learn from Source A? Circle your answer(s).

   i) Women were well treated in prison.

   ii) The Suffragettes wanted to gain the vote.

   iii) Women were force fed through a tube.   **[2]**

b) How reliable is the poster for understanding the aims of the Suffragette movement? Give reasons to show how it is and is not reliable in your answer.

_____

_____

_____

_____   **[4]**

c) Describe in your own words why this poster would be shocking to the public.

_____

_____

_____

_____   **[4]**

2 Study Sources A and B and then answer the questions that follow.

Source A: An article from the *Glasgow Herald* in 1914.

> Mrs Pankhurst was arrested at a women's suffrage demonstration in St Andrew's Hall, Glasgow, last night. Unparalleled scenes of disorder took place. The police stormed the platform, and for several minutes a fierce struggle ensued between them and Mrs Pankhurst's supporters, several persons being injured. Flower pots and chairs were thrown at the constables, who were obliged to draw their batons. In the course of the mêlée [confused hand-to-hand fight] the excitement was intensified by a woman firing several blank rounds from a revolver. When the suffragist leader was taken into custody Mrs Drummond addressed the meeting. Large crowds afterwards marched to the Central Police Station, where they were quickly dispersed by a strong force of constables.

Source B: A modern historian's view.

> Not all women agreed with the Pankhursts. There was even a Women's Anti-Suffrage League that campaigned to stop women getting the vote. They were doomed to failure and by 1928, all women over the age of 21 had the right to vote. Women had finally gained the same political rights as men.

a) Use Source A to describe three incidents of violence at St Andrew's Hall.

_____

_____ **[3]**

b) Which of these two sources is a secondary source? Give three reasons why the secondary source would be useful to a historian.

_____

_____

_____ **[3]**

c) Which source (A or B) would be most useful for a historian trying to find out about the Pankhursts?

_____

_____

_____

_____ **[4]**

Total Marks _____ / 20

Britain 1901–Present

The First World War

1 Describe what happened on 28th June 1914.

....

....

....

....

[2]

2 This photograph shows the site of Franz Ferdinand's assassination in Sarajevo, Bosnia.

Explain how the assassination of Franz Ferdinand, alliances, the arms race and empires led to the First World War.

Assassination of Franz Ferdinand: ....

....

....

Alliances: ....

....

....

Arms race: ....

....

....

Empires: ....

....

....

[8]

3 Study Source A and then answer the questions that follow.

Source A: A modern historian's view.

> There is no doubt that life in the trenches was grim. Disease, infestations and death were everywhere. Soldiers lived with the constant danger of enemy shelling, snipers and artillery bombardments. They were used to the death or injury of close friends, the dangers of poison gas attacks and living with rats and lice. They also endured a terrible diet of tea, biscuits and tinned beef. However it is also important to remember that soldiers were regularly rotated, and that the majority of their time was spent away from the frontline. The idea that soldiers spent months or years constantly in the trenches is a myth.

a) Which of the following can we learn from Source A? Circle your answer(s).

   i) There were rats in the trenches.

   ii) Most soldiers loved life in the trenches.

   iii) The trenches were dangerous. [2]

b) Name three risks to soldiers' lives listed in Source A.

   _____

   _____

   _____ [3]

c) Use Source A to write an account of what daily life in the trenches was like.

   _____

   _____

   _____

   _____

   _____ [5]

Total Marks _____ / 20

Britain 1901–Present

1 What date did *Kristallnacht* take place?

.... [1]

2 This photograph shows the inside of a concentration camp.

Name two infamous concentration camps.

....

.... [2]

3 How many Polish Jews died in the ghettos?

.... [1]

4 Explain the importance of *Kristallnacht* in relation to the treatment of Jews in Germany.
Give three reasons.

....

....

....

.... [3]

5 What happened to Jewish people during the 'Final Solution?' Give three examples.

....

....

....

.... [3]

6 Study Source A and then answer the questions that follow.

Source A: A newspaper report on the British evacuation from the beaches at Dunkirk, *Daily Mail*, 1 June 1940.

> An artillery man told me that with thousands of others he had spent two days among the sand dunes with little food and no shelter from the German dive bombers. Yet the men still joked, played cards, and even started a football game to keep up their spirits… A sailor told me that a vessel in which he had been assisting on the Belgian coast had been sunk. No sooner had he and his comrades landed in England than they all volunteered to go back at once.

a) Which of the following can we learn from Source A? Circle your answer(s).

   i) Soldiers spent two days on the beach.

   ii) Soldiers were never in danger.

   iii) Soldiers volunteered to carry on fighting.   **[2]**

b) Explain how reliable this source is, taking into account it is from a British newspaper.

    [3]

c) What can you learn about the evacuation of Dunkirk using Source A?

    [5]

Total Marks _____ / 20

Britain 1901–Present

The Creation of the Welfare State

1 Study Sources A and B and then answer the questions that follow.

Source A: A modern historian's view. (Note: Lloyd George was a liberal politician who held the belief that the government needed to intervene in the lives of the working classes to improve their health. The Labour Party wanted to attract the votes of the working class, which threatened the Liberals.)

> It would be naïve to assume that Lloyd George was motivated in his campaign of social reform mainly by compassion for the working classes. Primarily it was the emergence of the Labour Party and grave economic concerns that motivated him to improve the lives of the working class. Whilst his work showed progress, it did not go nearly far enough.

Source B: An election poster from 1906 campaigning for Keir Hardie to become a Labour MP.

VOTE FOR

Home Rule.
Democratic Government.
Justice to Labour
No Monopoly.
No Landlordism

Temperance Reform.
Healthy Homes.
Fair Rents.
Eight-Hour Day.
Work for the Unemployed.

KEIR HARDIE.

a) Study Source A. What are its strengths? What are its drawbacks?

_____

_____

_____

_____ **[4]**

b) Which source (A or B) is most reliable in showing the motivation behind Liberal welfare reform?

_____

_____

_____

_____

_____

_____ **[6]**

2 Study Sources A and B and then answer the questions that follow.

Source A: A modern historian's view. (Note: Aneurin Bevan was the creator of the NHS – National Health Service.)

> Many doctors opposed the NHS at first as they were concerned that they would be paid less, resented their taxes funding it and thought it was too expensive. They also felt it was not the government's job to interfere in people lives. Bevan was said to have 'stuffed their throats with gold' to get them to agree to work for the NHS.

Source B: A modern-day satirical [sarcastic/mocking] cartoon representing doctors' attitudes towards the NHS in the 1940s. Private practices on Harley Street stood to lose money under the NHS, so did not support it.

a) What four main reasons does Source A give for doctors' opposition to the NHS?

....

....

....

.... **[4]**

b) Which source (A or B) is most reliable in showing the problems Bevan faced when creating the NHS?

....

....

....

....

.... **[6]**

Total Marks .... / 20

Britain's Place in the World 1945–Present

1 Study Sources A and B and then answer the questions that follow.

Source A: A ration book from 1954.

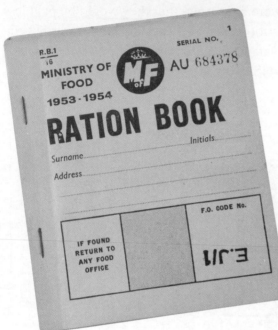

Source B: A modern historian's view.

Rationing of food and other goods during and after the Second World War changed the social landscape of Britain for a generation of people. It created a national culture of austerity, ingenuity and making do. Due to the harsh post-war conditions that resulted in a reduction in the availability of luxury goods and consumer goods, people had to become more inventive and creative with what they had. The public were only able to buy a limited amount of food each week. Items that were rationed included basic foods such as eggs, cheese, meat and sugar. Petrol and clothing were also rationed.

a) Use Source B to describe three effects of rationing.

....

....

.... **[3]**

b) Which of the sources is a secondary source? Give two reasons why this would be useful to a historian.

....

....

.... **[3]**

c) Use Sources A and B to describe what they tell you about post-war Britain.

....

....

....

.... **[4]**

2 Study Sources A and B and then answer the questions that follow.

Source A: A modern historian's view.

The emergence of teen culture in the 1960s changed Britain. Teenagers had previously listened to their parents' music of the 1940s. The Beatles and The Rolling Stones gave teenagers a sense of their own identity and helped to make attitudes more liberal, particularly towards women. The pill was introduced and abortion was legalised. They also had an influence on changing styles of dance and fashion. A musical and social revolution was born.

Source B: A London street in the 1960s.

a) Use Source A to describe three changes in society in the 1960s.

....

....

.... **[3]**

b) Study Source B and describe three ways in which it supports the information in Source A.

....

....

.... **[3]**

c) Which source (A or B) is more reliable for a historian trying to understand the social changes of the 1960s?

....

....

....

.... **[4]**

Total Marks .... / 20

British Social History

1 Give three reasons for the increase in emigration to Britain after 1945.

_____

_____

_____ **[3]**

2 Give three examples of discrimination the immigrants were subjected to. Explain your answer.

_____

_____

_____

_____

_____

_____ **[6]**

3 Write an account of what life was like for an immigrant in London in the 1950s.

_____

_____

_____

_____

_____ **[5]**

4 Study Sources A and B and then answer the questions that follow.

Source A: A modern historian's view.

The Irish faced a desperate situation. Millions were starving to death in Ireland and the British government was heavily criticised for failing to provide adequate help. However for those who emigrated life was still tough. The heath checks at Ellis Island in New York were both thorough and sometimes brutal. For those that made it through many faced a life of poor living conditions, disease and engrained racism.

Source B: A cartoon from *Harper's Weekly* (an American political magazine) entitled 'St. Patrick's Day 1867'.

a) Which of the following does Source A say faced the Irish on arrival in America? Circle your answer(s).

   i)   Guaranteed employment.

   ii) Poor living conditions.

   iii) Racism.   [2]

b) What impression does Source B give of the Irish?

   ....

   ....

   .... [3]

c) Use Sources A and B to write an account of what life was like for Irish migrants in America in the 19th century.

   ....

   ....

   ....

   ....

   .... [5]

Total Marks .... / 24

World History

USA in the 20th Century

1 What were the three key demands of the Civil Rights movement?

[3]

2 Outline the contribution of Martin Luther King to the Civil Rights movement.

[5]

3 Why did some white people still object to the integration of black people in the 1960s?

[2]

4 Study Sources A and B and then answer the questions that follow.

Source A: A modern historian's view.

> The strength of America's economy in the 1920s came to a sudden end in October 1929 – even if the signs of problems had existed before the Wall Street Crash. Suddenly the 'glamour' of the Jazz Age and gangsters disappeared and America was faced with a major crisis that was to impact countries as far away as Germany – a nation that had built its economy on American loans.

Source B: Front page of the *Daily Mail* newspaper announcing the Wall Street Crash, October 1929.

a) What does Source B suggest about the impact of the Wall Street Crash?

....

.... **[2]**

b) Which source is a primary source and why is this useful to a historian?

....

.... **[2]**

c) Use Sources A and B to describe in detail three important problems created by the Wall Street Crash.

....

....

....

....

....

.... **[6]**

Total Marks .... / 20

Mixed Test-Style Questions

Choose just one question to answer. Each question is worth 5 marks.

1 Study the source below on the routes of the Crusades.

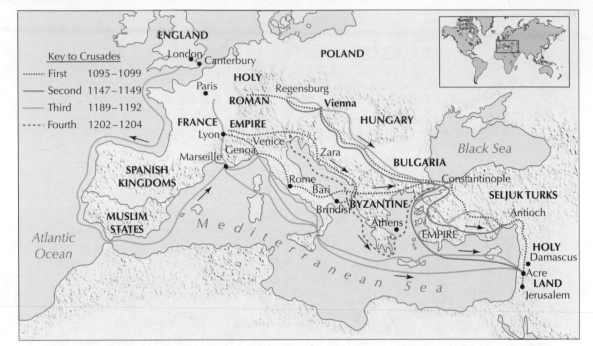

How is this source useful in helping you to explain why people might have wanted to go on a Crusade? How is it not useful?

Give reasons for your answer.

2 Study the source below, which is a modern historian's view about King John.

> The barons and King John did not like each other from the moment John became King. John interfered too much with how the country should be run. The barons believed that John needed to give more power to others.

Why does this source not give you enough information about why King John signed Magna Carta?

Give reasons for your answer.

Mixed Test-Style Questions

Choose just one question to answer. Each question is worth 5 marks.

1 Study the source below from approximately 1649, which shows the execution of Charles I in that year.

Use the source and your own knowledge to explain why the execution of the King was an important event.

2 Study the source below, which is a modern historian's view.

> The sheer brutality adopted by Charles to try to deal with his financial difficulties and growing objection to his rule horrified many. His use of the Court of the Star Chamber was widely considered to be illegal, especially with regard to punishing those unwilling to pay Ship Tax in inland areas. Punishments included cutting people's ears off, which was seen as a barbaric abuse of power.

Use this source and your own knowledge to explain how the issue of power contributed towards causing the English Civil War.

....

....

....

....

Mixed Test-Style Questions

Choose just one question to answer. Each question is worth 5 marks.

1 Study the source below, which is a modern historian's view.

> Cities were completely incapable of coping with the influx of population. Workers ended up being cramped into inadequate housing. Sewers were unable to cope and regularly overflowed. Many people did not have access to a clean water supply so infectious disease was rife.

Use this source and your own knowledge to explain the problems faced by workers in the cities in the industrial era.

In your answer, draw on your knowledge of epidemics and the concerns of reformers.

Support your answer with quotes from the source.

2 Study the source below, which is a modern historian's view.

> In 1831 there were riots in England when Parliament decided against reform that would have given Britain's industrial towns and cities better representation in Parliament and the vote to the working class. This decision led to widespread anger amongst the working class and numerous incidents of violence. In Nottingham people attacked the castle, home of the Duke of Newcastle. Protestors were arrested and some were executed. In Bristol protestors threw stones at the Mansion House, broke in and destroyed it, and three protestors were killed by police. The Bristol jail and Bishop's palace were also set on fire. In total an estimated 70 people died in the violence.

What useful information does this source give you about the working class at the time?

Include examples of violence and how the authorities dealt with it in your answer.

Choose just one question to answer. Each question is worth 5 marks.

1 Study the source below, which is a modern historian's view.

> The significance of the assassination of Archduke Franz Ferdinand has been widely disputed for many years. Some argue that if the crown prince of Austria had not been assassinated by a Serbian terrorist in 1914 the First World War would not have broken out. Others argue that war in Europe was inevitable in the early 20th century as tensions surrounding empires, arms and alliances reached boiling point.

Use this source and your own knowledge to discuss the importance of the Archduke Franz Ferdinand's assassination in causing the First World War.

In your answer you should weigh up the importance of the assassination against other causes of the war.

Support your answer with quotes from the source.

2 Study Sources A and B and then answer the question that follows.

Sources A: An extract from Winston Churchill's speech in 1940.

Source B: A poster quoting Winston Churchill.

> The gratitude of every home in our island, in our Empire, and indeed throughout the world, except in the abodes of the guilty, goes out to the British airmen who, undaunted by odds, unwearied in their constant challenge and mortal danger, are turning the tide of the world war by their prowess and by their devotion. Never in the field of human conflict was so much owed by so many to so few.

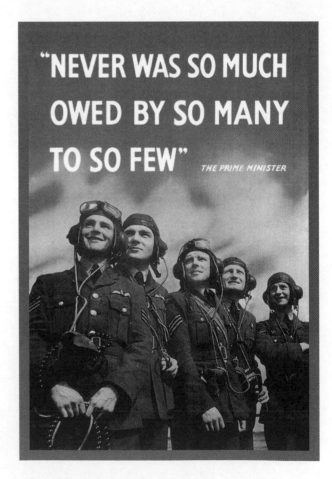

Use both sources to explain why the Battle of Britain in 1940 was a pivotal event.

Mixed Test-Style Questions

Choose just one question to answer. Each question is worth 5 marks.

1 Study the source below, which is a modern historian's view.

> The government recognised the need to rebuild Britain following the air raids of the Second World War. In addition to this there was an increased need for workers following the creation of the NHS in 1948. The government saw recruitment from the Empire as the ideal solution to Britain's shortage of workers. In addition to this many soldiers from the Empire had fought alongside British soldiers during the war, which it believed would help integration.

Use this source and your own knowledge to explain why and how the government encouraged emigration to the UK in the post-war years.

In your answer you should include details of government Acts to encourage immigration and explain why there was a need for workers.

Support your answer with quotes from the source.

2 Study Sources A and B and then answer the question that follows.

Sources A: Rosa Parks on a bus.

Source B: A modern historian's view.

> By the early 1960s there had been some progress in desegregating schools, and the Montgomery bus boycott had raised awareness of the fight for equality. However in many Southern states black Americans were still treated as second-class citizens. Throughout the campaign Martin Luther King urged the civil rights movement to continue with non-violent protest.

Use both sources and your own knowledge to explain why Rosa Parks and Martin Luther King believed in non-violent protest.

....

....

....

....

....

Mixed Test-Style Questions

Choose just one question to answer. Each question is worth 10 marks.

1 How did William consolidate his power after the Battle of Hastings?

Support your answer with evidence.

2 Imagine you are a peasant who has survived the Black Death.

Write an account of how life has changed. Include a discussion of both economic and social factors.

3 Why was the Peasants' Revolt not successful in 1381?

Support your answer with evidence.

Mixed Test-Style Questions

Choose just one question to answer. Each question is worth 10 marks.

1 Why do you think slavery was eventually abolished in Britain?

Support your answer with evidence.

2 The Industrial Revolution is regarded as a turning point in English history.

Give your own opinion as to why it is important.

Support your answer with evidence.

3 Explain why the formation of the Suffragist movement in 1897 was a significant development for women attempting to gain the vote.

In your answer you should give your opinion on at least three different reasons.

Support your answer with evidence.